Historical Sketch And Roster Of The North Carolina 4th Infantry Regiment Senior Reserves

Not all of a people are privileged by nature to brave the dangers of war and enjoy its glory, but true loyalty may be as strongly manifested by those who remain at home and perform those duties essential to the maintenance of the military force.

By John C. Rigdon

Historical Sketch And Roster Of The North Carolina 4th Infantry Regiment Senior Reserves

10th Printing – FEB 2019 8/1/4/2

Published by:
Eastern Digital Resources
31 Bramblewood Dr SW
Cartersville, GA 30120
http://www.researchonline.net
EMAIL: Sales@Researchonline.net
Tel. (678) 739-9177

Contents

A Turtle On A Fence Post

If You ever see one, you'll know he didn't get there by himself.

This work has been compiled from a number of different sources. I have concentrated on firsthand accounts and primary sources when available. It is my hope that this sketch will help in your research and become the basis of future in depth research into this regiment and the men who served.

If you have additional information on the men who served in this unit, or the regiment's actions in battle, drop me a note at JRigdon@researchonline.net. I will incorporate them into future editions.

Aye, But Its Hopes Are Dead

Sir Henry Houghton - England

Sir Henry Houghton, of England, in 1865, wrote these beautiful lines as a reply to "The Conquered Banner." The Southern people never expect to see that sacred banner unfurled except to typify the noblest deeds of the human race.

Gallant nation, foiled by numbers,
Say not that your hopes are fled;
Keep that glorious flag which slumbers,
One day to avenge your dead.
Keep it, widowed, sonless mothers,
Keep it, sisters, mourning brothers,
Furl it with an iron will;
Furl it now, but keep it still,
Think not that its work is done.
Keep it till your children take it,
Once again to hail and make it
All their sires have bled and fought for,
Bled and fought for all alone.
All done! aye, shame the story,
Millions here deplore the stain;
Shame, alas! for England's glory,
Freedom called, and called in vain.
Furl that banner, sadly, slowly,
Treat it gently, for 'tis holy,
Till that day---yes, furl it sadly,
Then once more unfurl it gladly,
Conquered banner, keep it still.

Officers

Colonel:

- John F. Hoke

Major:

- John N. Prior

Lt. Colonel:

- Leroy W. Stowe

Brigade/Division/Corps Commanders

Col. John K. Connally

Connally's Brigade of North Carolina Reserves

(600 men in late December, 1864)

4th Battalion North Carolina Junior Reserves
Cos. A, B, C, D, Maj. John M. Reece
7th Battalion North Carolina Junior Reserves
Cos. A B, C, Maj. William F. French
8th Battalion North Carolina Junior Reserves
Cos. A, B, C, Maj. James Ellington
8th North Carolina Senior Reserves Cos. B, C, D, E, F,
Col. Allmond McKoy

The 4th North Carolina Regiment Senior Reserves were added to this brigade in January, 1865.

Captain James C. Cooper, Jr., a Confederate veteran of Henderson, N. C., was born in Granville county in 1841, a son of Alexander Cooper. The latter, who was a son of James Cooper, a native of Scotland, was a prosperous planter, and was in the Confederate service as a member of the Senior reserves. Captain Cooper was educated at the Hillsboro military academy, and in the spring of 1861 enlisted in the Granville Grays, which was assigned as Company I to the Second regiment, North Carolina troops. On May 5, 1861, he was transferred to the Eighth regiment and promoted to lieutenant. While a member of this command he was captured at Roanoke island and after a short imprisonment on board a Federal steamship was paroled, and in September, 1861, was exchanged. In December, 1862, he was commissioned as captain commissary of the Second North Carolina cavalry, commanded by Col. Sol Williams, and he served with this regiment until after the Gettysburg campaign. Returning then to his lieutenancy in the Eighth regiment he was appointed, after the battle of Cold Harbor, assistant inspector-general of Clingman's brigade, in which capacity he served until the close of the war. With the Second cavalry he was in battle at Brandy Station, Hanover, Carlisle and Gettysburg; in 1864 met the advancing army at Cold Harbor, and subsequently shared the services of Clingman's brigade at Drewry's bluff, Petersburg, Wilmington, Kinston and Bentonville, finally being paroled at High Point, N.C. After the conclusion of hostilities Captain Cooper was engaged in the cotton and commission business at New York city for twelve years or more, and then entered the tobacco trade, first at Oxford, N. C., and since 1885 at Henderson.

Source: Confederate Military History Vol. IV pg. 450

Companies

The companies of the 4th Senior Reserves were formed from the 3rd Military District in January of 1865.

Assignments

Mounted patrol guard for the Northwestern North Carolina counties.

Assigned to Connally's Brigade, Senior Reserves, 3rd Military District, Department of North Carolina (Jan-Feb 1865)

Synopsis

The North Carolina 4ᵗʰ Infantry Regiment Senior Reserves was also known as the 73ʳᵈ Infantry Regiment North Carolina Troops. The 4ᵗʰ Reserves do not appear in the Official Records.

The regiment was organized in early 1865 and participated in the Carolina's campaign. It surrendered as part of the Army of TN at Durham Station, Orange Co, NC April 26, 1865.

As the name implies, the Senior Reserves were made up of older men and men who were unfit to serve in the regular army. Unlike the militia and "home guards" however, these men were in actual Confederate Service acting primarily as provost guards, railroad guards and operators, and pickets at bridges and forts.

The 4ᵗʰ Senior Reserves served as mounted patrol guard for the Northwester North Carolina counties.

Historical Sketch

Very little is known of the North Carolina Senior Reserve Units. A total of 5,618 men were enrolled in 8 units according to D. H. Hill in Confederate Military History. My rosters of these units have a total of 5,237 names:

NC 2nd Infantry Regiment Senior Reserves – 2

NC 3rd Infantry Battalion Senior Reserves – 362

NC 4th Infantry Regiment Senior Reserves – 984

NC 5th Infantry Regiment Senior Reserves – 1100

NC 6th Infantry Regiment Senior Reserves – 955

NC 7th Infantry Regiment Senior Reserves – 938

NC 8th Infantry Regiment Senior Reserves – 874

Hart's Company NC Senior Reserves – 7

McCorkle's Battalion NC Senior Reserves – 17

The 4th Infantry Regiment Senior Reserves was also known as the 73rd Infantry Regiment North Carolina Troops. It was organized in early 1865 and participated in the Carolina's campaign. It surrendered as part of the Army of TN at Durham Station, Orange Co, NC 04/26/1865. The 4th Reserves does not appear in the Official Records.

Most of the senior reserve units served as prison guards at Salisbury, North Carolina. Few of the men actually wanted to be in service, and many were AWOL when a muster roll was prepared on February 28, 1865.

I have found no record of a 1st Senior Reserves and the 2nd obviously has something approaching 1,000 names which are unknown. I think we can also estimate Hart's Company at 100 men and McCorkle's Battalion at 500, so on the one hand, Gen. Hill's number may be low by 1,200 men and my rosters may also need another 1,500 or so names.

A remarkable proof of the State's brave devotion to the Confederacy is noteworthy in this connection. As shown by the census of 1860, the total number of men in North Carolina between the ages of 20 and 60, the extreme limits of military service, was 128,889. Subtract from this number the number of troops furnished, and it reveals the extraordinary fact that in the whole of North Carolina there were only 3,889 men subject to military duty who were not in some form of martial service. Most of these 3,889 were exempted because they were serving the State in civil capacity, as magistrates, county officers, dispensers of public food, etc. So, practically, every man in the State was serving the State or the Confederacy. It may well be doubted whether a more striking evidence of public devotion was ever recorded.

As the name implies, the Senior Reserves were made up of older men and men who were unfit to serve in the regular army. Unlike the militia and "home guards" however, these men were in actual Confederate Service acting primarily as provost guards, railroad guards and operators, and pickets at bridges and forts.

The 5th regiment was formed by the consolidation of two battalions in the summer of 1864. It is reasonable to place the formation of the higher numbered units at the same time.

On March 10, 1864, Erwin's Battalion of Senior Reserves is listed as serving under Gen. J. G. Martin and J. B. Palmer's Brigade. Gen. J. G. Martin had been recalled from the Virginia army and placed in command of the Western department of North Carolina, with headquarters at Asheville. These regiments of active, hardy mountaineers were mainly employed in repelling the numerous raids through the mountains by Federal mixed forces, and in meeting detachments from Col. George W. Kirk's notorious regiment of Union North Carolinians. This regiment was a constant menace to that section and was restlessly energetic. In July, 1864, it surprised and captured Camp Vance, near Morganton. Into this camp about 200 Junior reserves had been assembled to be mustered into the Confederate service. Only one company had arms, and the surprise was so complete that this company could not fire a shot. Kirk made off with his captures. At Winding Stairs a few regular and local troops overtook and attacked him, but he made good his escape with his prisoners. In this engagement Col. W. W. Avery was mortally, and Col. Calvin Houk, seriously wounded.

To meet the raiders, and, in many cases, marauders of that section, General Martin directed Maj. A. C. Avery, of Hood's staff, then at home on account of family reasons, to organize a new battalion to operate against them. This little battalion, composed of Capt. John Carson's company, of McDowell, Capt. N. A. Miller's company, of Caldwell, and

Capt. W. L. Twitty's company, of Rutherford county, rendered most faithful service in keeping deserters and marauders out of their counties. In March, Colonel Kirk entered Haywood county, but Colonel Love, of the Sixty-ninth regiment, met him at Balsam Grove and drove him back. On March 5, 1865, Colonel Kirk encamped on the headwaters of the Saco with part of his command. The next morning Lieutenant-Colonel Stringfield, also of the Sixty-ninth regiment, attacked him with some Indian and white companies of the Thomas legion. During the time of Stoneman's raid into the mountains, all the troops there were more or less engaged. Near Morganton a little field piece served by Lieut. George West and some soldiers on furlough, and supported by Captain Twitty, of Avery's battalion and Maj. T. G. Walton of the militia, bravely held in check for some hours one of Stoneman's detachments.

Most of the accounts of the Senior Reserve units in the existing records do not identify which unit(s) were involved. Where records do exist, I have included them in this book, but some of these may require detailed research to determine which unit was involved. The references I have found specific to the 4th Regiment indicate that were rolled into the Army of Tennessee shortly after organization in January of 1865 and they participated in the Carolina's Campaign from that time until the surrender. They were assigned to Connally's Brigade which had arrived at Fort Fisher on Dec. 26, 1864 just after the engagement of Dec. 24th & 25th. The men of the 4th may have been involved in this garrison support in which 224 men of the reserves were captured by the 117th New York. No casualties were reported in either killed or wounded.

Sherman's March Through The Carolinas

Gen. Sherman's march through South Carolina began in late December, 1864. By 9 MAR 1865, his troops had passed out of the state into North Carolina - leaving behind a path of total destruction 100 miles wide and extending the entire length of the state.The campaign began in late November 1864 even before the surrender of Savannah, but due to the strong resistance by Gen. Wheeler's Cavalry, Sherman's first troops did not cross the river into South Carolina until 15 January 1865. He had reported to his superiors that he expected the Carolina march to last 4 to 5 weeks, but in fact it was late March before his troops passed out of South Carolina into North Carolina. He later reported that his march had not begun until the end of January.

"We marched backwards all the way to Goldsboro" was how one of the old men who were a part of the SC Militia remembered the period. The remnant of the Army of Tennessee, once again under the command of Gen. Joseph E. Johnston, Gen. Wheeler's Cavalry, State Militia units of boys and older men, and various SC commands relieved from duty in Virginia in order to protect their own farms, opposed and hindered Gen. Sherman's march at every step.

Gen. Sherman's troops generally regarded the people of South Carolina with contempt. In his journal, dated 26 FEB 1865, Thomas Osborn of the Federal Artillery gave this account:

"These men are the most contemptible crowd I have ever seen used as soldiers. Most of them are old, gray headed men, from fifty to sixty-five years of age, many of them have heads as white as snow, and nearly all of them are infirm; there are a few small boys among them. We shall be compelled to parole most of them as they will be unable to march with the Army, and we have not transportation for them. Humanity would demand that these old cripples and little children be all carried in ambulances."[1]

Indeed, the confederate forces were a motley crew, but they had hearts of steel. The Mayor of Columbia reported that "there were not 1,400 able bodied men left in the entire state of South Carolina to defend against Gen. Sherman's march."[2] Indeed, by this time, South Carolina had lost over 20,000 of her men to the war - fully one third of the men between ages 16 and 50 having been killed for the cause.

When they left Savannah, Federal troop strength was 60,000 consisting of the 14th, 15th, 17th, and 20th Army Corps plus a Cavalry Corps of 4,000. Each of the Federal Army Corps consisted equally of about 13,000 men. Throughout the march, each army took a slightly different route in a swath 100 miles wide from Savannah and Beaufort, SC to Columbia, then northeast towards Fayetteville, NC.

The total Confederate troops involved were 33,400, although not all of them were available to defend the state in the early part of the campaign. I estimate that at most about 5,000 Confederate forces were in the state in early January, 1865. The remnants of the Hood's Army were in Tennessee following the terrible loss at Nashville on 15 - 19 DEC 1864. Gen. Hood resigned on 13 JAN 1865, and Gen. Johnston once again resumed command and led the men from Tennessee to

South Carolina. The troops passed through Augusta in late January, repairing the railroad as they went, and by late January had approx 30,000 troops in the mid-state with about 20,000 being fit for battle.

The loss of life both to the Confederate and Federal armies, and the population at large was relatively light in view of the destruction of property. In his report, the Surgeon for the Federal Forces, D. L. Huntington, puts their losses at 106 deaths and 697 wounded. A tally of the first hand accounts indicates a much higher number - something approaching 1,000 deaths. Confederate casualties are unknown for this period. There is a report of some 200 civilians being massacred in the upstate above Columbia, and something less than 20 killed when Columbia was burned, but the records are virtually non-existent as Sherman burned almost everything in his path. The tallies made by the federal officers would indicate approx. 300 confederate troops died.

The following excerpts are taken from "The Fiery Trail" by Thomas Osborn and other first hand accounts of the march.

30 DEC 1864 - Exit Savannah

02 JAN 1865 - First Crossing into South Carolina by Federal Troops

05 JAN 1865 - Pocotaligo

09 JAN 1865 - Sherman and his officers arrived by Steamer at Beaufort from Savannah. They met the XV and XVII A.C. which had marched out of Savannah on 31 DEC 1864. "I do

not think it is in General Sherman's plans to move directly against Charleston, but to neutralize it by other operations. It is strongly fortified and an attempt to take it would result in a large loss of men. The information we pick up indicates that the enemy is not in large force in this part of the country, but that the main body of the troops have been shipped to some other point. The prominent railroad connections above us, the possession of which appear to be of value in cutting off supplies from General Lee's army are Branchville, Columbia, Florence, Raleigh, Goldsboro, Greensboro, Weldon and Danville.." [3] "Our soldiers were so many, needed so many supplies, and felt themselves at last on South Carolina soil, that a lawless spirit came over them and many complaints came to me of their doings." [4]

14 JAN 1865 - Gen. Howard leaves Beaufort to join Gen. Blair and the XV A.C. Battle at Pocotaligo creek. Federal loss - 2 officers killed and 2 men wounded. Federal forces take the railroad at Pocotaligo Station with a loss of about a dozen men.

15 JAN 1865 - Right wing of Sherman's army reaches Beaufort, SC

17 JAN 1865 - XVII A.C. occupies the Savannah & Charleston railroad. Loss Federal - about 12 men. "The XVII Corps has occupied the Charleston and Savannah railroad which it succeeded in doing with a loss of about a dozen men. I am told here that at one time and another 6,000 men have been lost in attempts to occupy this railroad from this point. Of course we have more men than has at any one time been employed and the enemy are in less confident spirit than at any time before. Yet I am disposed to think that the success

with so light a loss is more owing to good military judgment than to any other cause." [5]

25 JAN 1865 - 4 straight days of rain reported - all streams uncrossable. Federal estimates up to 20,000 Confederate in front. "We are about starting on a new campaign and it is not now unlikely we shall be absent from the coast as long as we were between Atlanta and Savannah. We may not be out of reach more than two weeks, quite likely six, but I guess about four. We cannot tell how much the enemy will oppose us, from present indications not very much, but probably more then [sic] in the last campaign. General Grant notifies General Sherman that General Lee shall not send his army, or any portion of it, against this. If that promise can be kept, the enemy has not force enough in our front to hinder us greatly.[6]

26 JAN 1865 - The XV A.C. leaves Beaufort. "We know little or nothing about the future. General Sherman says it is to be the greatest campaign yet undertaken. So General Hooker said before Chancellorsville, and he was correct. I hope General Sherman will not be correct in the same sense."[7]

28 JAN 1865 - Roper's Crossroads

29 JAN 1865 - Federal forces leave Pocataligo for the mid-state. Federal troop strength 60,000 men. Gen. Slocum has crossed the Savannah River above Savannah and is moving towards Branchville. "The remnants of General Hood's army, left after the battle of Nashville, is moving east and will probably be in our front again." [8]

02 FEB 1865 - Rivers' Bridge - Salkehatchire River. Federal losses about a dozen men killed and wounded. Confederate dead reported by Federal forces - four. "We took last evening seven prisoners, and this morning picked up a few more. We learn that the 5th, 37th, 47th Georgia Infantry Regiments were here also 5th South Carolina Artillery, 4th Tennessee Cavalry, also two companies of Texas Cavalry, in all 2700 men, commanded by Colonel Harrison, 32nd Ga. Infantry."9 "At McBride's plantation, where Sherman had his headquarters, the out-houses, offices, shanties, and surroundings were all set on fire before he left. I think the fire approaching the dwelling hastened his departure... In Georgia few houses were burned; here few escaped, and the country was converted into one vast bonfire. The pine forests were fired; the resin factories were fired; the public buildings and private dwellings were fired. The middle of the finest day looked black and gloomy, for a dense smoke rose on all sides clouding the very heavens - at night the tall pine trees seemed so many huge pillars of fire. The flames hissed and screeched, as they fed on the fat resin and dry branches, imparting to the forest a most fearful appearance... The ruins of homesteads of the Palmetto State will long be remembered. The army might safely march the darkest night, the crackling pine woods shooting up their columns of flame, and the burning houses along the way would light it on, while the dark clouds and pillars of smoke would safely cover its rears. I hazard nothing in saying that three-fifths of value of the personal property of the counties we passed through were taken by Sherman's army." 10

03 FEB 1865 - Federal forces reach the Salkahatchie river. "The actual invasion of South Carolina has begun... The well-known sight of columns of black smoke meets our gaze

again; this time houses are burning, and South Carolina has commenced to pay an installment, long overdue, on her debt to justice and humanity. With the help of God, we will have principal and interest before we leave her borders. There is a terrible gladness in the realization of so many hopes and wishes. This cowardly traitor state, secure from harm, as she thought, in her central position, with hellish haste dragged her Southern sisters into the caldron of secession. Little did she dream that the hated flag would again wave over her soil; but this bright morning a thousand Union banners are floating in the breeze, and the ground trembles beneath the tramp of thousands of brave Northmen, who know their mission, and will perform it to the end." [11]

05 FEB 1865 - Branchville "The majority of the citizens here are of the same "cracker or sand hill" species we have found so plentiful everywhere we have been. I heard a soldier say to his comrade today the "the whole damned state was not worth the life of our Federal soldiers," He was about right. We everywhere hear the fear expressed of "Negro equality," while no one ever expressed a fear of equality with this class of "Southern white trash." They are lower than the negro in every respect, not excepting general intelligence, culture, and morality. A man not acquainted with this larger population of the South can form an idea of it in their style of living and cleanliness, &c. They are not fit to be kept in the same sty with a well to do farmer's hogs in New England. Once in ten or fifteen miles we find a plantation owned by a "reliable" man, a "first family" who lives in Charleston or Columbia, while every half mile we find a shanty with the poles a foot apart, a stick chimney, three or four half naked children, two or three with nothing but a shirt, but with an incrustation of dirt which entirely conceals

the natural color; the mother with her person partially concealed by ragged cotton cloth and dirt combined. If you ask her where her husband is, the reply is "in the Army"... [12]

07 FEB 1865 - Blackville "Our foraging parties are now gathering on the north side of the river more material than can be consumed, and large accumulations will be left in the morning... we find more supplies in this country than I feared we might. Chickens, sweet potatoes, fresh pork, and honey and fresh lard, all rewarded the zealous inquiries of our headquarters foragers today." [13] "Our troops reached the R.R. about 2 P.M. .. There is a German Jew who has a couple hundred bales of cotton and wants protection because he is a foreigner. He asks that his cotton be saved to pay some "beebles" [people] up in New York, who he owes some "little debts." He will hardly save the cotton. "[14] "I visited today the residence of William Gilmore Simms, the South Carolina novelist and author of "Marion" &c. He has evacuated but has left a very ardent secesh family to protect the residence and library for him. He has a fine library. I think it will be saved, but I should have no objection to seeing it burned... many books from his library, bearing his autograph, found their way into camp, and were carried away by the men as mementoes." [15]

11 FEB 1865 - North Fork - Orangeburg "We do so many thing that are wrong in this living off the country in the way we do that I do not like it and I am afraid of retribution...but the army must be fed and the Bummers must feed us,"[16]

11 FEB 1865 - Battle of Aiken

12 FEB 1865 - Orangeburg "Orangeburg contains about 800 people, and was, before we entered it a fine little place with a fair proportion of churches, small cotton brokers' establishments, &c &c... If the town had been built on purpose for a bonfire it could not have been bettered. All that could be done was to watch it on the windward side and the outskirts of the town. We occupied the town at 2 P. M. and at four one third or one half of the town was on fire and burning with the greatest rapidity. I think one half of the body of the town was destroyed. The fires was not so extensive as the one in Atlanta, but more grand and beautiful."17

13 FEB 1865 - Big Beaver Creek "Today has been beautiful, clear and still. From the starting of the column this morning we could trace the tracks of each by the column of smoke from burning buildings, cotton, turpentine mills, pine woods &c. [Along] the line of the XVII A.C. on the R. R. the smoke lifted like a grand curtain here and there, tassled by a more dense column of smoke from a store house of cotton or resin. The columns of smoke which marked Logan's line of march were more isolated, but in themselves were very dense. Many of these columns were really wonderful. The smoke rising from the pitch fields rolled up in volumes to the sky so impenetrable that not a ray of light could be seen through them. They looked like a dozen cities burning at the same time. I wish I had the power of describing the grandeur of this scene." 18

15 FEB 1865 - Little Congaree

16 FEB 1865 - Saluda Factory on the Saluda River "A little before midnight last night the enemy opened fire from a

battery in position on the north side of the river, firing into the rear of our troops on this side. We had no artillery with which we could silence it and they did considerable damage, killing an officer and several men, and wounding nearly twenry. The fire was very annoying." [17]

17 FEB 1865 - Gen. Hampton evacuates Columbia

18 FEB 1865 - Columbia surrendered to the Federal forces - subsequently burned. "... when the brigade occupied the town the citizens and negroes brought out whiskey in buckets, bottles and in every conceivable manner treated the men to all they would drink. ... The negroes, escaped prisoners, state convicts, and such other people as would all went into the work of pillaging with a will. By this time all parties were willing to assist it on... The negroes piloted the men to the best places for plunder, and both men and negroes by evening were setting fires rapidly... One cannot conceive of anything which would or could make a grander fire than this one, excepting a larger city than Columbia. The city was built entirely of wood, and was in most excellent condition to burn. The space on fire at midnight was not less than one mile square, and one week before, sheltered from 25,000 to 30,000 people. The flames rolled and heaved like the waves of the ocean; the road was like a cataract. The whole air was filled with burning cinders, and fragments of fire as thick as the flakes of snow in a storm. The scene was splendid - magnificently grand. The scene of pillaging, the suffering and terror of the citizens, the arresting of and shooting negroes, and our frantic and drunken soldiers... this I will leave for the present for the imagination of those who choose to dwell upon it... I have in this war seen too much... and choose rather to remember the magnificent

splendor of this burning city... I believe the burning of the city is an advantage to the cause and a just retribution to the state of South Carolina. [20]

21 FEB 1865 - Winnsboro "Two of our men were found today with their brains beat out, and from all appearances had been captured and then murdered." [21]

23 FEB 1865 - Rocky Mount "General Sherman sends us word again today that the enemy have murdered eleven of Kilpatrick's men, and the General has also ordered retaliation by killing the same number of rebels now in Kilpatrick's hands. Kilpatrick reported the incident: " An infantry lieutenant and seven men murdered yesterday by the 8th Texas Cavalry after they had surrendered. We found their bodies all together and mutilated, with paper on their breasts, saying "Death to foragers." Eighteen of my men were killed yesterday and some had their throats cut... I have sent Wheeler word that I intend to hang eighteen of his men... I have a number of prisoners and shall take a fearful revenge." [22]

02 MAR 1865 - Cheraw

02 MAR 1865 - Florence "The sufferings which the people will have to undergo will be most intense. We have left on the wide strip of country we have passed over no provisions which will go any distance in supporting the people. We have left no stock by means of which they can get more. All horses, mules and cattle, sheep and hogs have been taken. They cannot go outside of the country traversed for lack of transportation... Even before we came into the State the provisions were vastly greater than we had ever supposed...

We have been out on this trip a little longer than before, and made the same distance, and covered the same or a greater breadth of territory, and have again left nothing... I do not think that the Rebel armies will not fight, they will do so whenever an opportunity offers, which affords a hope of success. They still believe their government, their property, their honor, and their Southern pride is at stake, and they will fight for them. "In addition to what is said above of the people, there is one thing they invariably do, no matter how great the cost: they cling to the niggers as the visible proof of their respectability and chivalry and no matter how great the sacrifices they are compelled to make to restore them, they willingly make the sacrifices.23

11 MAR 1865 - Fayetteville, NC

16 MAR 1865 - Averasboro

19 MAR 1865 - Bentonville

26 APR 1865 - Gen. Johnston's troops surrendered at Goldsboro, NC

NOTES:

1. Osborn, Thomas. The Fiery Trail - A Union Officer's Account of Sherman's Last Campaigns. Knoxville, The University of Tennessee Press. 1986 pg. 143.

2. ibid. pg.

3. ibid. pg. 81.

4. Howard, Oliver Otis. Autobiography. 2 vols. New York: D. Appleton & Co. 1907. pg. 98-99.

5. Osborn. pg. 82

6. ibid. pg. 83

7. ibid. pg. 83

8. ibid. pg. 85

9. ibid. pg. 101

10. ibid. pg. 103

11. ibid. pg. 100

12. ibid. pg. 102

13. ibid. pg. 104

14. ibid. pg. 108

15. Simms, William Gilmore. Sack and Destruction of the City of Columbia. SC Atlanta 1937. pg. 18-19.

16. Howard. Collection of personal papers in a letter to his daughter. 17. Osborn. pg. 117.

18. ibid. pg. 119.

19. ibid. pg. 125.

20. ibid. pg. 128.

21. ibid. pg. 143

22. O. R. Ser. 1 vol. 47 pt. 2 pg. 533.

23. Osborn. pg. 153.

Col. Hoke's Command at Williamsburg.

[Col. Hoke, commander of the 4th Senior Reserves was Adjutant General of North Carolina in 1861. He assumed command of the 13th North Carolina State Troops which became the 23rd Infantry Regiment in 1862. The following account of the battle of Williamsburg on May 5, 1862 was written by H. C. Wall and published in the Raleigh, N. C., News and Observer, April 11, 1897.]

On the night of the 3d of May Yorktown was evacuated. Twelve miles out in the suburbs of the ancient town of Williamsburg the battle of the 5th of May occurred, rendered necessary by the too eager pursuit of the enemy. From a point on the road several miles beyond the town towards Richmond, Early's Brigade - now composed of the 5th and 23d North Carolina, the 24th Virginia and the 2d Florida Battalion – was ordered back to aid Longstreet in resisting the furious attack. At the moment of our reaching the field the bloody drama was going on in full view of the town. Much was said at the time and afterwards of the part the 23d Regiment took in that battle. The writer can only give facts from a personal standpoint, as recalled by him, a private then in ranks, conscious too of a liability to error in an understanding of the existing facts. The design was a charge by Early's Brigade against a strong position manned by Hancock's Brigade, on the enemy's right. When drawn up in line for the forward movement, General Early rode the length of the brigade, using, in that fine-toned voice of his, something like the words: "Boys, you must do your duty." The line had steadily advanced a 100 yards or more when a body of thick forest of trees and undergrowth confronted the 23d, into which the regiment marched, the line at once becoming irregular and more or less jumbled by reason of the natural obstacles to its progress. At this moment General

D. H. Hill appeared, mounted, in our front, and saying sharply to the men, now confused in ranks and each one commanding his comrades: "Hush your infernal noise." In an instant more the right wing of the brigade, having greatly the advantage of ground in marching, as we believe, and thus coming first in view of the enemy's battery, received their galling fire, and was hurled back by a fury of shot and shell irresistible by mortal force. The 5th North Carolina made a gallant but fruitless charge, losing many valuable lives, and the 23d did not support it at the critical moment. That moment was of the briefest possible span; like a sea wave against the sea wall, the charge bounded back instantly. Colonel D. K. McRae, of the 5th North Carolina, alleged that the 23d was inexcusably derelict in duty, and that its colonel halted the regiment in those woods without authority. Colonel Hoke, on the contrary, maintained that General Early gave the order to halt. Whether the command of "halt" and "lie down" was given to the 23d a second sooner than the batteries opened on the assaulting columns, would be hard to tell, for the action of the 23d in halting and lying down appeared to be about the same moment a portion of the assaulting force was rushing pell-mell back upon its line in the woods. It was all the work of a few minutes, and the brigade, chagrined at defeat and mourning the loss of many gallant spirits, fell back in order. Only four or five men in the 23d were wounded, and this by random bullets.

General Joseph E. Johnston, in a conversation with the writer several years after the war, placed the responsibility for this charge upon General D. H. Hill. He said he did not order it made, but permitted it only, however, after repeated requests from General Hill. The enemy seemed content to hold his own, without much further effort to advance his line as the shades of night came on.

During the night and early dawn of the 6th the grand retreat was resumed. The 6th of May found the army on the march without a mouthful to eat, as the wagons had gone far ahead towards Richmond. On the evening of the 9th the Chickahominy was reached, and here the wagons were overtaken, much to the delight of drooping hearts and hungry stomachs. On this day, while bivouacked on the banks of the river, the reorganization of companies in the 23d Regiment took place, and new regimental officers were elected, as follows: Daniel H. Christie, Colonel; Robert D. Johnston, former captain of Company K, Lieutenant-Colonel; Ed. J. Christian, former lieutenant of Company C, Major; Vines E. Turner, former lieutenant of Company G, Adjutant.

Leo D. Heartt

Leo D. Heartt, cashier of the First national bank of Durham, in his boyhood was earnestly devoted to the Confederate cause and served as a clerk in the office of Gov. Zebulon B. Vance. It was his special duty to carry messages from the governor and to act as a courier between the executive department and officers in the field, and in this capacity he frequently went through the lines and obtained a vivid impression of the circumstances of war. He carried the last dispatches from the governor to the headquarters of Gen. Wade Hampton, and accompanied the governor on a personal visit to that distinguished commander. Subsequently he was engaged in mercantile pursuits, until he became connected with the banking business at Raleigh, where he remained until 1887, when, upon the organization of the First national bank at Durham, he was invited to accept the position of cashier. He is also a director of the Durham & Northern railroad. He has taken an active part in municipal affairs, as alderman for several terms and as chairman of the graded school committee. For twelve years he served as assistant paymaster-general of the State military organization. Mr. Heartt is a native of Raleigh and a son of Leo E. Heartt, a prominent merchant who served during the war with the Senior reserves. His grandfather, Dennis Heartt, a native of Connecticut, of German descent, was at the time of his death the oldest newspaper editor in the country. Mr. Heartt was married in 1872 to Annie, daughter of Oliver S. Dewey, collector of the port at New Bern during the war, and after the evacuation of that place, in charge of the commissary department.

Source: Confederate Military History Vol 4 pg. 536.

James H. Lassiter

James H. Lassiter, a prominent businessman and patriotic citizen of Henderson, N. C., was born in Gates county, May 27, 1816, a son of Blake Lassiter. In 1842 Mr. Lassiter first embarked in business as a merchant in Murfreesboro, N.C. During the war his age prevented him from rendering active service in the field, but he was thoroughly devoted to the cause, and is yet loyal to the memory of the brave boys who served in the North Carolina regiments. He rendered duty when called upon as a member of the Senior reserves, [3rd NC Battalion Senior Reserves, Co. A] and in the commissary department did efficient service in gathering and furnishing supplies to the army. Not all of a people are privileged by nature to brave the dangers of war and enjoy its glory, but true loyalty may be as strongly manifested by those who remain at home and perform those duties essential to the maintenance of the military force. Among these latter Mr. Lassiter is worthy of remembrance. Since 1865 he has been very successfully engaged in business at Henderson, is a director of the Citizens bank, and of the storage warehouse and cotton mill, and in various channels of activity is an enterprising and valuable citizen.

Source: Confederate Military History Vol 4 pg. 536.

James K. Wood

James K. Wood, of Oxford, N. C., a veteran of the naval service of the Confederate States, was born at Oxford July 31, 1844, a son of James M. Wood, who was a member of the Senior reserves of North Carolina and is yet living (1898) at Berea, Granville county. In 1862 Mr. Wood entered the Confederate States service on board the ironclad North Carolina, and was on duty with this vessel about two years. Subsequently he was attached to the ironclad Raleigh, under the command of Lieut. Pembroke Jones. He was on board the Raleigh when she steamed out of Cape Fear river, in May, 1864, escorting blockade-runners. She drove several Federal vessels out to sea, but on her return up the river stuck upon the bar and went to pieces. After this Mr. Wood was on duty on a battery below Fort Fisher, on the North Carolina until she went to pieces, later in the Battery Cameron, near Wilmington, and after the evacuation of that city was on duty at Drewry's bluff until the abandonment of the Confederate capital. He was a member of the party under command of Col. John Taylor Wood, which, in the early part of February, 1864, made a night assault upon the United States steamer Underwriter in the Neuse river, at New Bern, N.C. The surprise and capture of this Federal vessel was one of the most daring exploits of the war and elicited a joint resolution of thanks from the Confed-erate Congress. Since the close of hostilities Mr. Wood has been very successfully engaged in business at Ox-ford, and is a highly respected and influential citizen.

Source: Confederate Military History Vol 4 pg. 536.

Field Staff and Band

Hoke, John F. - Rank in Colonel. Rank out Colonel. From Richmond County. Adjutant General for North Carolina in 1861. Colonel of the NC 13th Infantry Regiment when organized in the spring of 1861. On the reorganization of the regiment in 1862, and the redesignation as the 23rd Infantry, Col. Hoke was succeeded by D. H. Christie.

John F. Hoke, son of Col. John Hoke, won a captain's commission in the Mexican War, and commanded his company with gallantry in the battles of Cerro Gordo, Tolema and National Bridge. He was adjutant • general in North Carolina and colonel in the civil War. He was an able lawyer, and often the representative of Lincoln county in the General Assembly. His son, William A. Hoke, as citizen, lawyer, legislator, judge of the Superior Court, and now Associate Justice of the Supreme Court, occupies a large space in public esteem

REF: http://www.lelawhisnant.net/journeysthrutime/id107.htm

Stowe, Leroy W. - Rank in Lieutenant Colonel. Rank out Lieutenant Colonel. At the battle of 2nd Manassas and at Gettysburg he is listed as a Captain in the North Carolina 16th Infantry Regiment.

Prior, John N. - Rank in Major. Rank out Major.

Phifer, George L. - Rank in Private Company F. Rank out Acting Commissary of Subsistence.

Around 1850, Andrew Motz and E.S. Barrett built the Laurel Hill Cotton  Factory near the confluence of the South Fork River and Clark's Creek, one mile west of Lincolnton. About 1858, Col. John Fulenwider Phifer and Col. R.W. Allison, cousins from Concord, North Carolina, purchased the property and operated it as the Ivy Shoals Cotton Mill. Col. John F. Phifer married Elizabeth Caroline

Ramsour, daughter of David Ramsour, a Lincolnton merchant, on June 5, 1839, and established his home in Lincolnton in 1842 after working as a planter in Lowndes County, Georgia. Phifer's wealth was well known throughout the county, as he was one of the largest slave owners in Lincoln County during the 1860s. During this period, when citizens referred to other wealthy persons in the county, they used the expression, "He is almost as wealthy as Col. Phifer."[3] Upon the death of Col. Phifer in 1884, his son, George L. Phifer, and son-in-law, Stephen Smith, of Livingston, Alabama, operated the mill until Robert S. Reinhardt became a partner in 1890 and changed the name to Elm Grove Cotton Mill.[1]

The only cotton mill in the county at the close of the war was the **Elm Grove,** owned by John F. Phifer, now operated by Robert S. Reinhardt.[2]

Waring, Robert P. - Rank in Adjutant. Rank out Adjutant.

---

[1]
http://www.lincolncountyhistory.com/projects/eureka/eureka.html

[2] http://www.ncgenweb.us/lincoln/ncl_nixon.htm

Company A

Sain, Chesire - Rank in Captain. Rank out Captain.

Clifford, John W. - Rank in First Lieutenant. Rank out First Lieutenant.

Clinton, DeWitt - Rank in Second Lieutenant. Rank out Second Lieutenant.

Allen, James H. - Rank in Private. Rank out Private.

Allen, Johruty S. - Rank in Private. Rank out Private.

Bailey, Sanford - Rank in Private. Rank out Private.

Barnacastle, Elijah - Rank in Private. Rank out Private.

Beck, Wilson - Rank in Private. Rank out Private.

Blackwell, Robert - Rank in Private. Rank out Private.

Blum, George A. - Rank in Private. Rank out Private.

Brackin, R. D. - Rank in Private. Rank out Private.

Chaplin, Solomon - Rank in Private. Rank out Private.

Clifford, James - Rank in Private. Rank out Private.

Cranfill, Alex - Rank in Private. Rank out Private.

Crawly, Jackson - Rank in Private. Rank out Private.

Davis, George C. - Rank in Private. Rank out Private.

Downs, William R. - Rank in Private. Rank out Private.

Drake, Green - Rank in Private. Rank out Private.

Dyson, Tilmon - Rank in Private. Rank out Private.

Dyson, William - Rank in Private. Rank out Private.

Eaton, B.H. - Rank in Private. Rank out Private.

Faircloth, Thomas - Rank in Private. Rank out Private.

Fry, Hannon - Rank in Private. Rank out Private.

Garawood, Nathaniel - Rank in Private. Rank out Private.

Glasscock, Thomas N. B. - Rank in Private. Rank out Private.

Graves, Wilson - Rank in Private. Rank out Private.

Gullet, James - Rank in Private. Rank out Private.

Hamline, George - Rank in Private. Rank out Private.

Heath, Milbourn - Rank in Private. Rank out Private.

Helton, L. G. - Rank in Private. Rank out Private.

Hillard, James - Rank in Private. Rank out Private.

Hillard, William - Rank in Private. Rank out Private.

Houser, James - Rank in Private. Rank out Private.

Houser, James - Rank in Private. Rank out Private.

Howard, David - Rank in Private. Rank out Private.

Howard, William - Rank in Private. Rank out Private.

Howard, Wilson - Rank in Private. Rank out Private.

Ijames, William J. - Rank in Private. Rank out Private.

Jackson, William F. - Rank in Private. Rank out Private.

Jones, Cullen - Rank in Private. Rank out Private.

Jones, P. L. - Rank in Private. Rank out Private.

Jones, Samuel - Rank in Private. Rank out Private.

Jones, Spencer - Rank in Private. Rank out Private.

Kerfeese, C. S. - Rank in Private. Rank out Private.

Kerfeese, Martin - Rank in Private. Rank out Private.

Lambert, John C. - Rank in Private. Rank out Private.

Lane, Duglass - Rank in Private. Rank out Private.

Langston, William H. - Rank in Private. Rank out Private.

Lefler, John A. - Rank in Private. Rank out Private.

Lowder, Mathias - Rank in Private. Rank out Private.

McCulloh, James - Rank in Private. Rank out Private.

McDaniel, Joseph - Rank in Private. Rank out Private.

Miller, Jacob C. - Rank in Private. Rank out Private.

Miller, William - Rank in Private. Rank out Private.

Mumford, G. E. - Rank in Private. Rank out Private.

Murphy, Basil - Rank in Private. Rank out Private.

Myers, John - Rank in Private. Rank out Private.

Naylor, John W. - Rank in Private. Rank out Private.

Nelson, J. B. - Rank in Private. Rank out Private.

Orrell, James - Rank in Private. Rank out Private.

Owens, Joel - Rank in Private. Rank out Private.

Parks, Mack - Rank in Private. Rank out Private.

Parsons, J. B. - Rank in Private. Rank out Private.

Pickler, A. F. - Rank in Private. Rank out Private.

Presley, Andrew - Rank in Private. Rank out Private.

Queen, Mitchel - Rank in Private. Rank out Private.

Richardson, Columbus - Rank in Private. Rank out Private.

Seaford, Simeon - Rank in Private. Rank out Private.

Seamont, James - Rank in Private. Rank out Private.

Sloan, Samuel - Rank in Private. Rank out Private.

Smith, Anderson W. - Rank in Third Lieutenant. Rank out Second Lieutenant.

Smith, J. A. - Rank in Private. Rank out Private.

Smith, L. G. - Rank in Private. Rank out Private.

Smith, S. O. - Rank in Private. Rank out Private.

Smith, William - Rank in Private. Rank out Private.

Spry, Lemuel - Rank in Private. Rank out Private.

Spry, William - Rank in Private. Rank out Private.

Tatum, E.W. - Rank in Private. Rank out Private.

Taylor, John - Rank in Private. Rank out Private.

Tisenger, Peter - Rank in Private. Rank out Private.

Tutterow, H. - Rank in Private. Rank out Private.

Tutterow, Samuel - Rank in Private. Rank out Private.

Tutterow, W.W. - Rank in Private. Rank out Private.

Walker, T.E. - Rank in Private. Rank out Private.

Williams, Isaac - Rank in Private. Rank out Private.

Williams, Martin - Rank in Private. Rank out Private.

Willson, D. C. - Rank in Second Lieutenant. Rank out Second Lieutenant.

Wright, John L. - Rank in Private. Rank out Private.

Company B

Atwell, James A. - Rank in Corporal. Rank out Corporal.

Baker, James T. - Rank in Private. Rank out Private.

Barger, Martin - Rank in Private. Rank out Private.

Basinger, Charles - Rank in Private. Rank out Private.

Bostian, Jacob - Rank in Sergeant. Rank out Sergeant.

Brawley, John M. - Rank in Captain. Rank out Captain.

Brown, John D. - Rank in Private. Rank out Private.

Brown, William M. - Rank in Private. Rank out Private.

Casper, David - Rank in Corporal. Rank out Corporal.

Casper, Levi - Rank in Private. Rank out Private.

Cauble, Isaac - Rank in Private. Rank out Private.

Christie, John A. - Rank in Private. Rank out Private.

Clodfelter, George A. - Rank in Private. Rank out Private.

Clodfelter, John F. - Rank in Private. Rank out Private.

Coleman, John M. - Rank in Private. Rank out Private.

Coon, George - Rank in Private. Rank out Private.

Correll, Levi - Rank in First Lieutenant. Rank out First Lieutenant.

Cozart, Hiram W. - Rank in Private. Rank out Private.

Cristy, John A. - Rank in Private. Rank out Private.

Cruse, Charles A. - Rank in Private. Rank out Private.

Deal, John - Rank in Private. Rank out Private.

Douherty, David - Rank in Private. Rank out Private.

Eagle, David - Rank in Private. Rank out Private.

Eckler, Almon - Rank in Private. Rank out Private.

Eller, Michael - Rank in Private. Rank out Private.

Ellis, Willis - Rank in Private. Rank out Private.

Ernheart, Henry - Rank in Private. Rank out Private.

Estes, Irvin - Rank in Private. Rank out Private.

File, Tobias - Rank in Private. Rank out Private.

Fraley, Thomas D. - Rank in Private. Rank out Private.

Freeze, John L. - Rank in Private. Rank out Private.

Goodman, George - Rank in Private. Rank out Private.

Graham, William - Rank in Private. Rank out Private.

Harkey, George - Rank in Private. Rank out Private.

Hauser, William H. - Rank in Private. Rank out Private.

Holshouser, Jacob - Rank in Private. Rank out Private.

Holshouser, John - Rank in Private. Rank out Private.

Hyde, John S. - Rank in Private. Rank out Private.

Jacobs, William W. - Rank in Private. Rank out Private.

Jameson, John E. - Rank in Private. Rank out Private.

Kesler, Tobias - Rank in Private. Rank out Private.

Kincade, Andrew J. - Rank in Private. Rank out Private.

Klutz, Simeon - Rank in Private. Rank out Private.

Klutz, Solomon - Rank in Private. Rank out Private.

Knox, David F. - Rank in Private. Rank out Private.

Krider, George H. - Rank in Private. Rank out Private.

Krider, Leonard S. - Rank in Second Lieutenant. Rank out Second Lieutenant.

Lamb, Alexander - Rank in Private. Rank out Private.

Lawrence, Levi - Rank in First Sergeant. Rank out First Sergeant.

Leazer, John W. - Rank in Private. Rank out Private.

Linfield, J.W. - Rank in Private. Rank out Private.

Linfield, James - Rank in Private. Rank out Private.

Link, John W. - Rank in Private. Rank out Private.

Litaker, Michael - Rank in Private. Rank out Private.

Long, Peter - Rank in Private. Rank out Private.

Lyerly, George M. - Rank in Private. Rank out Private.

Lyerly, William A. - Rank in Second Lieutenant. Rank out Second Lieutenant.

Lytaker, Michael - Rank in Private. Rank out Private.

Mahaley, Jesse A. - Rank in Private. Rank out Private.

McKnight, John - Rank in Sergeant. Rank out Sergeant.

McLaughlin, John H. - Rank in Private. Rank out Private.

McLean, John W. - Rank in Private. Rank out Private.

Menus, Henry - Rank in Private. Rank out Private.

Miller, Charles - Rank in Sergeant. Rank out Sergeant.

Miller, John - Rank in Private. Rank out Private.

Miller, Michael - Rank in Private. Rank out Private.

Mills, William J. - Rank in Private. Rank out Private.

Morgan, Jacob - Rank in Private. Rank out Private.

Morgan Jr., Wiley - Rank in Private. Rank out Private.

Morgan Sr., Wiley - Rank in Private. Rank out Private.

Morrison, John L. - Rank in Private. Rank out Private.

Mowery, Alexander - Rank in Private. Rank out Private.

Murph, Jeffrey - Rank in Private. Rank out Private.

Overcash, Leonard - Rank in Private. Rank out Private.

Pace, Abner - Rank in Private. Rank out Private.

Page, William - Rank in Private. Rank out Private.

Pahel, John - Rank in Private. Rank out Private.

Peeber, George H. - Rank in Private. Rank out Private.

Penniger, Nelson - Rank in Private. Rank out Private.

Pethel, John - Rank in Private. Rank out Private.

Pethel, Levi A. - Rank in Private. Rank out Private.

Petrea, Augustus - Rank in Private. Rank out Private.

Petrie, Augustus - Rank in Private. Rank out Private.

Phillips, Andrew J. - Rank in Private. Rank out Private.

Pool, Edward - Rank in Private. Rank out Private.

Powlass, John - Rank in Private. Rank out Private.

Rex, William - Rank in Private. Rank out Private.

Rimer, Caleb - Rank in Private. Rank out Private.

Roseman, James O. - Rank in Private. Rank out Private.

Rusher, Milas - Rank in Sergeant. Rank out Private.

Rusher, Miles - Rank in Sergeant. Rank out Private.

Rymer, Caleb - Rank in Private. Rank out Private.

Shaver, Daniel - Rank in Private. Rank out Private.

Shepperd, James A. - Rank in Private. Rank out Private.

Sherford, Daniel D. - Rank in Private. Rank out Private.

Shipping, Moses - Rank in Corporal. Rank out Corporal.

Shoaf, Alexander - Rank in Private. Rank out Private.

Shuping, Caleb - Rank in Corporal. Rank out Corporal.

Shuping, Moses - Rank in Corporal. Rank out Corporal.

Sossaman, H. M. - Rank in Private. Rank out Private.

Sterritt, James L. - Rank in Private. Rank out Private.

Stirewalt, Adam - Rank in Private. Rank out Private.

Sulliman, John P. - Rank in Private. Rank out Private.

Traley, Thomas D. - Rank in Private. Rank out Private.

Trexler, Moses - Rank in Private. Rank out Private.

Trott, Jackson - Rank in Private. Rank out Private.

Upright, John - Rank in Private. Rank out Private.

Upright, Samuel S. - Rank in Private. Rank out Private.

Upwright, John - Rank in Private. Rank out Private.

Waggoner, John - Rank in Private. Rank out Private.

Weaver, John M. - Rank in Private. Rank out Private.

Wilhelm, Henry - Rank in Private. Rank out Private.

Williams, John - Rank in Private. Rank out Private.

Woodruff, William L. - Rank in Private. Rank out Private.

Company C

Abernathy, Milton - Rank in Private. Rank out Private.

Angel, Abel - Rank in Private. Rank out Private.

Balch, Hiram - Rank in Private. Rank out Private.

Ballard, Elisha - Rank in Corporal. Rank out Corporal.

Ballard, John - Rank in Private. Rank out Private.

Ballard, John F. - Rank in Private. Rank out Private.

Ballinger, Michael - Rank in Second Lieutenant. Rank out Second Lieutenant.

Barger, Thomas - Rank in Private. Rank out Private.

Barkely, Robert - Rank in Private. Rank out Private.

Bumgarner, Aman - Rank in Private. Rank out Private.

Burch, T. F. - Rank in Private. Rank out Private.

Burress, Ezekiel - Rank in Private. Rank out Private.

Carpenter, John - Rank in Private. Rank out Private.

Caulter, Eli S. - Rank in Private. Rank out Private.

Claninger, John - Rank in Private. Rank out Private.

Cline, Aman - Rank in Private. Rank out Private.

Cook, Johnson - Rank in Private. Rank out Private.

Coons, John - Rank in Private. Rank out Private.

Danner, Alexander - Rank in Private. Rank out Private.

Davis, James L. - Rank in Private. Rank out Private.

Deal, Franklina - Rank in Private. Rank out Private.

Deal, L. A. - Rank in Private. Rank out Private.

Deitz, Caleb - Rank in Private. Rank out Private.

Deitz, Lazarus - Rank in Private. Rank out Private.

Edwards, John - Rank in Private. Rank out Private.

Edwards, Sparhart - Rank in Private. Rank out Private.

Finger, John - Rank in Private. Rank out Private.

Fisher, Coleman - Rank in Private. Rank out Private.

Frazier, Alex - Rank in Private. Rank out Private.

Fry, Salaman - Rank in Private. Rank out Private.

Fullbright, David - Rank in Private. Rank out Private.

Fullbright, Henry - Rank in Private. Rank out Private.

Haller, Andrew - Rank in Sergeant. Rank out Sergeant.

Haller, Franklin - Rank in Private. Rank out Private.

Haller, Peter - Rank in Private. Rank out Private.

Hartman, James - Rank in Private. Rank out Private.

Hauk, Harrison - Rank in Private. Rank out Private.

Hawn, Jesse - Rank in Private. Rank out Private.

Hawn, John - Rank in Private. Rank out Private.

Hayle, H. H. - Rank in First Sergeant. Rank out First Sergeant.

Herman, George - Rank in Private. Rank out Private.

Hicks, C. P. - Rank in Private. Rank out Private.

Horwell, Horace - Rank in Private. Rank out Private.

Huffman, Jackson - Rank in Private. Rank out Private.

Huffman, Martin - Rank in Private. Rank out Private.

Huit, M.M. - Rank in Corporal. Rank out Corporal.

Hunsucker, Lawson - Rank in Private. Rank out Private.

Isenhaur, Isaac - Rank in Private. Rank out Private.

Johnson, A.L. - Rank in Private. Rank out Private.

Kahill, Daniel - Rank in Private. Rank out Private.

Kale, Henderson - Rank in Private. Rank out Private.

Keener, Daniel - Rank in Private. Rank out Private.

Lael, Jacob - Rank in Private. Rank out Private.

Lare, Ephraim - Rank in Private. Rank out Private.

Linebarger, H.H. - Rank in Sergeant. Rank out Sergeant.

Linn, Archebald - Rank in Private. Rank out Private.

Love, F. G. - Rank in Private. Rank out Private.

Lynn, Archibald - Rank in Private. Rank out Private.

Marshall, John - Rank in Private. Rank out Private.

Matthews, Levi - Rank in Private. Rank out Private.

Matthews, Peter - Rank in Private. Rank out Private.

McClemmer, George - Rank in Private. Rank out Private.

Meadlock, Elijah - Rank in Private. Rank out Private.

Miller, W.F. - Rank in Private. Rank out Private.

Mingus, Miles - Rank in Private. Rank out Private.

Poovey, Emanuel - Rank in Private. Rank out Private.

Pope, Aman - Rank in Private. Rank out Private.

Propst, Ales - Rank in Private. Rank out Private.

Propst, Avery - Rank in Private. Rank out Private.

Propst, Michael - Rank in Private. Rank out Private.

Rhoney, John G. - Rank in Private. Rank out Private.

Seitz, D.D. - Rank in Private. Rank out Private.

Setzer, David - Rank in Private. Rank out Private.

Setzer, James H. - Rank in Corporal. Rank out Corporal.

Sherrill, J.S. - Rank in Private. Rank out Private.

Sherrill, James - Rank in Private. Rank out Private.

Shook, Daniel - Rank in Private. Rank out Private.

Shook, David - Rank in Private. Rank out Private.

Shook, Jacob - Rank in Private. Rank out Private.

Shuford, Max - Rank in Private. Rank out Private.

Sigman, Abel - Rank in Private. Rank out Private.

Sigman, David - Rank in Private. Rank out Private.

Sigman, Emanuel - Rank in Junior Second Lieutenant. Rank out Second Lieutenant.

Sigman, Lanson - Rank in Private. Rank out Private.

Simmon, Daniel - Rank in Private. Rank out Private.

Simmon, Joel - Rank in Private. Rank out Private.

Smith, Marcus M. - Rank in Captain. Rank out Captain.

Speagle, Emanuel - Rank in Private. Rank out Private.

Spencer, Eli - Rank in Sergeant. Rank out Sergeant.

Turner, B.S. - Rank in Private. Rank out Private.

Whitener, A. J. - Rank in Private. Rank out Private.

Whitener, Abel - Rank in Private. Rank out Private.

Whitener, Z. B. - Rank in Private. Rank out Private.

Woodring, Joseph - Rank in Corporal. Rank out Corporal.

Wyckoff, Abraham - Rank in First Lieutenant. Rank out First Lieutenant.

Wycoff, Abram - Rank in First Lieutenant. Rank out First Lieutenant.

Yaunt, F. A. - Rank in Sergeant. Rank out Sergeant.

Company D

Anderson, J. C. - Rank in Private. Rank out Private.

Barnard, Thomas - Rank in Private. Rank out Private.

Barnsley, W.H. - Rank in Private. Rank out Private.

Bass, John - Rank in Private. Rank out Private.

Bedman, T. - Rank in Private. Rank out Private.

Benfield, Frederic - Rank in Private. Rank out Private.

Bost, John - Rank in Private. Rank out Private.

Bostian, John - Rank in Private. Rank out Private.

Brady, R. A. - Rank in Private. Rank out Private.

Brandon, N. H. - Rank in Private. Rank out Private.

Brawley, J. G. - Rank in Private. Rank out Private.

Brawley, N. S. - Rank in Private. Rank out Private.

Brown, A. - Rank in Private. Rank out Private.

Brown, T. - Rank in Private. Rank out Private.

Brown, T. A. - Rank in Private. Rank out Private.

Calvert, R. S. - Rank in Private. Rank out Private.

Campbell, T. M. - Rank in Private. Rank out Private.

Carr, Charles - Rank in Private. Rank out Private.

Carter, N. - Rank in Private. Rank out Private.

Christian, George W. - Rank in Private. Rank out Private.

Click, J.G. - Rank in Private. Rank out Private.

Collins, Henry - Rank in Private. Rank out Private.

Condy, William F. - Rank in Junior Second Lieutenant. Rank out Second Lieutenant.

Crawford, W.R. - Rank in Private. Rank out Private.

Cruse, G.B. - Rank in Private. Rank out Private.

Current, A. - Rank in Private. Rank out Private.

Dancey, Enos - Rank in Private. Rank out Private.

Daywalt, William - Rank in Private. Rank out Private.

Dishman, William - Rank in Private. Rank out Private.

Dunkan, Harvey - Rank in Private. Rank out Private.

Eagh, G.A. - Rank in Private. Rank out Private.

Edmonds, J. H. – Name not in the National Archives Index. From Columbus County.

REF: tparker1@triad.rr.com (great great grandson)

Edwards, J.W. - Rank in Private. Rank out Private.

Ervwin, Adolphus - Rank in Private. Rank out Private.

Ervwin, J.H. - Rank in Private. Rank out Private.

Fowler, J. W. - Rank in Private. Rank out Private.

Freeland, T.A. - Rank in Private. Rank out Private.

Freeland, Thomas A. - Rank in Private. Rank out Private.

Freis, Daniel - Rank in Private. Rank out Private.

Gaither, J.J. - Rank in Private. Rank out Private.

Gaither, Martin - Rank in Private. Rank out Private.

Gibson, Felix - Rank in Private. Rank out Private.

Gibson, Fishling - Rank in Private. Rank out Private.

Goforth, Thomas B. - Rank in Private. Rank out Private.

Grant, John - Rank in Private. Rank out Private.

Gray, H. M. - Rank in Private. Rank out Private.

Gregory, M. - Rank in Private. Rank out Private.

Gross, William - Rank in Private. Rank out Private.

Guthery, N.C.R. - Rank in Private. Rank out Private.

Guthry, Martin - Rank in Private. Rank out Private.

Hair, D.J. - Rank in Private. Rank out Private.

Haire, D.J. - Rank in Private. Rank out Private.

Hampton, F.H. - Rank in Private. Rank out Private.

Harris, Henry - Rank in Private. Rank out Private.

Hays, W. - Rank in Private. Rank out Private.

Heathcock, James - Rank in Private. Rank out Private.

Henry, G. H. - Rank in Private. Rank out Private.

Hobbs, H. - Rank in Private. Rank out Private.

Holland, Nathaniel - Rank in Private. Rank out Private.

Howard, Pinkey - Rank in Private. Rank out Private.

Hudson, H. - Rank in Private. Rank out Private.

Huithcox, T.A. - Rank in Private. Rank out Private.

Ireland, Amos - Rank in Private. Rank out Private.

Keaton, Silas - Rank in Private. Rank out Private.

Kennerly, J. P. - Rank in Private. Rank out Private.

Kimball, H.M. - Rank in Private. Rank out Private.

Kimball, Thomas - Rank in Private. Rank out Private.

King, C.H. - Rank in Private. Rank out Private.

Knox, D.J.L. - Rank in Private. Rank out Private.

Lamberth, John - Rank in Private. Rank out Private.

Lambirth, W.L. - Rank in Private. Rank out Private.

Lantham, T. - Rank in Private. Rank out Private.

Lawson, R.E. - Rank in Private. Rank out Private.

Lazenberry, E.P. - Rank in Private. Rank out Private.

Lazenberry, H.B. - Rank in Private. Rank out Private.

Lazenberry, R.M. - Rank in Private. Rank out Private.

Leach, L. - Rank in Private. Rank out Private.

Lenty, D. - Rank in Private. Rank out Private.

Lyerly, C. - Rank in Private. Rank out Private.

Mason, T. M. - Rank in Private. Rank out Private.

Mathiason, Henry - Rank in Private. Rank out Private.

Mayer, R. M. - Rank in Private. Rank out Private.

Mayes, Rufus W. - Rank in Private. Rank out Private.

McClelland, J. M. - Rank in Private. Rank out Private.

McClelland, - Rank in Private. Rank out Private.

McConnell, Thomas - Rank in Private. Rank out Private.

McCorkle, G. R. - Rank in Private. Rank out Private.

McCrarry, John S. - Rank in Private. Rank out Private.

McCrary, T. F. - Rank in Private. Rank out Private.

McNeely, J.E. - Rank in Private. Rank out Private.

Merkin, J. - Rank in Private. Rank out Private.

Miller, W.G. - Rank in Private. Rank out Private.

Miner, John - Rank in Private. Rank out Private.

Minish, J. C. - Rank in Private. Rank out Private.

Misenheimer, M. - Rank in Private. Rank out Private.

Monteith, Abner - Rank in Private. Rank out Private.

Moore, Robert - Rank in Private. Rank out Private.

Morrison, F. - Rank in First Lieutenant. Rank out First Lieutenant.

Morrison, Thomas G. - Rank in Captain. Rank out Captain.

Morrison, William F. - Rank in First Lieutenant. Rank out First Lieutenant.

Morrow, Stephen - Rank in Private. Rank out Private.

Mullis, Williams - Rank in Private. Rank out Private.

Myars, James - Rank in Private. Rank out Private.

Myers, Jeremiah - Rank in Private. Rank out Private.

Myers, Rufus W. - Rank in Private. Rank out Private.

Neil, W. S. - Rank in Private. Rank out Private.

Nicholson, E. - Rank in Private. Rank out Private.

Overcash, Caleb - Rank in Private. Rank out Private.

Overcash, James - Rank in Private. Rank out Private.

Overcash, S. - Rank in Private. Rank out Private.

Overcash, William - Rank in Private. Rank out Private.

Parker, A. - Rank in Private. Rank out Private.

Pasten, Thomas - Rank in Private. Rank out Private.

Perry, Joseph - Rank in Private. Rank out Private.

Plyler, Hugh - Rank in Private. Rank out Private.

Plyler, L. - Rank in Private. Rank out Private.

Posten, John E. - Rank in Second Lieutenant. Rank out First Lieutenant.

Poston, John E. - Rank in Second Lieutenant. Rank out First Lieutenant.

Privy, Joseph - Rank in Private. Rank out .

Ramsy, William H. - Rank in Private. Rank out .

Renager, Nathan - Rank in Private. Rank out .

Rusher, Milas - Rank in Sergeant. Rank out Private.

Rusher, Miles - Rank in Sergeant. Rank out Private.

Scofield, J.N. - Rank in Private. Rank out .

Scott, A.M. - Rank in Private. Rank out .

Sharpe, David - Rank in Private. Rank out .

Snider, D. - Rank in . Rank out .

Snyder, Daniel - Rank in Private. Rank out .

Sprinkle, Moses - Rank in Private. Rank out .

Stack, J. - Rank in Private. Rank out Private.

Stack, Jerry - Rank in Private. Rank out .

Steele, James - Rank in Private. Rank out .

Stephenson, W. S. - Rank in Private. Rank out .

Summers, B.F. - Rank in Private. Rank out .

Tanner, H. - Rank in Private. Rank out .

Thompson, Henry - Rank in Private. Rank out .

Thrap, Thomas - Rank in Private. Rank out .

Tom, D.C. - Rank in Private. Rank out .

Tomlin, J.H. - Rank in Private. Rank out .

Vaughn, A. - Rank in Private. Rank out .

Wagoner, J.L. - Rank in Private. Rank out .

Wagoner, Len F. - Rank in Private. Rank out .

Walker, William - Rank in Private. Rank out .

Wallace, J.C. - Rank in Private. Rank out .

Watts, J. A. - Rank in Private. Rank out .

Waugh, B. A. - Rank in Private. Rank out .

Weatherman, Henry H. - Rank in Second Lieutenant. Rank out Second Lieutenant.

Westmoreland, - Rank in Private. Rank out .

Wharton, J. - Rank in Private. Rank out .

White, Alex - Rank in Private. Rank out .

White, B. - Rank in Private. Rank out .

Whitehead, Jesse - Rank in Private. Rank out .

Wilhelm, A. D. - Rank in Private. Rank out .

Wilkson, D. - Rank in Private. Rank out .

Willford, W. H. - Rank in Private. Rank out .

Williams, Alex. - Rank in Private. Rank out .

Williams, M. - Rank in Private. Rank out .

Williams, S. - Rank in Private. Rank out .

Wooton, J. - Rank in Private. Rank out .

Wooton, L. W. - Rank in Private. Rank out .

Wright, W. - Rank in Private. Rank out .

Company E

Abernathy, C. B. - Rank in Private. Rank out Private.

Abernathy, Charles B. - Rank in Private. Rank out Private.

Abernathy, D. M. - Rank in Private. Rank out Private.

Armstrong, John M. - Rank in Private. Rank out Private.

Armstrong, Mathew R. - Rank in Private. Rank out Private.

Armstrong, Thomas - Rank in Private. Rank out Private.

Baldon, William - Rank in Private. Rank out Private.

Black, Daniel - Rank in Second Lieutenant. Rank out Second Lieutenant.

Blackwood, John - Rank in Private. Rank out Private.

Bogen, Halden - Rank in Private. Rank out Private.

Bookout, Levi - Rank in Private. Rank out Private.

Brown, Philip W. - Rank in Private. Rank out Private.

Burke, Monroe - Rank in Private. Rank out Private.

Carpenter, Abel - Rank in Private. Rank out Private.

Carpenter, Alfred - Rank in Private. Rank out Private.

Carpenter, W.B. - Rank in Private. Rank out Private.

Clemmer, Adam - Rank in Private. Rank out Private.

Costner, Joseph - Rank in Private. Rank out Private.

Cox, Patrick - Rank in Private. Rank out Private.

Dillen, William - Rank in Private. Rank out Private.

Falls, And. J. - Rank in Private. Rank out Private.

Fore, James M. - Rank in Private. Rank out Private.

Fromberger, Ambrose - Rank in Private. Rank out Private.

Gant, A.J. - Rank in Private. Rank out Private.

Gaston, Robert - Rank in Private. Rank out Private.

Gaston, Robert H. - Rank in Private. Rank out Private.

Glenn, Stanhope - Rank in Private. Rank out Private.

Harvey, James N. - Rank in Private. Rank out Private.

Hill, William R. - Rank in Private. Rank out Private.

Hoffman, David - Rank in Private. Rank out Private.

Hoffman, Jacob - Rank in Private. Rank out Private.

Holman, Ambrose - Rank in Private. Rank out Private.

Holman, Jacob - Rank in Private. Rank out Private.

Homsley, Amos B. - Rank in Private. Rank out Private.

Hoover, Thomas - Rank in Private. Rank out Private.

Horsley, Richard - Rank in Private. Rank out Private.

Horton, Richard - Rank in Private. Rank out Private.

Jenkins, Berryman - Rank in Private. Rank out Private.

Lewis, James - Rank in Private. Rank out Private.

Lineberger, Jonas R. - Rank in Private. Rank out Private.

Lockhart, William - Rank in Private. Rank out Private.

Lowrance, M. C. - Rank in Private. Rank out Private.

Manney, John - Rank in Private. Rank out Private.

McAlister, David - Rank in Private. Rank out Private.

McAlister, Elisha - Rank in Private. Rank out Private.

McCarver, Eli - Rank in Private. Rank out Private.

McElwain, John - Rank in Private. Rank out Private.

McIlvane, John - Rank in Private. Rank out Private.

McLure, William C.D. - Rank in Private. Rank out Private.

McNair, James - Rank in Private. Rank out Private.

Merril, Martin S. - Rank in Private. Rank out Private.

Mooney, John - Rank in Private. Rank out Private.

Morrison, William P. - Rank in Private. Rank out Private.

Morrisson, Evan T. - Rank in Private. Rank out Private.

Morrisson, John - Rank in Private. Rank out Private.

Nims, Harris - Rank in Private. Rank out Private.

Pasour, Felix - Rank in Private. Rank out Private.

Penglase, Richard - Rank in Private. Rank out Private.

Plonk, David - Rank in Third Lieutenant. Rank out Second Lieutenant.

Plunk, David - Rank in Third Lieutenant. Rank out Second Lieutenant.

Ramsey, Jacob - Rank in Private. Rank out Private.

Rankin, Robert - Rank in Private. Rank out Private.

Ransey, Jacob - Rank in Private. Rank out Private.

Reid, James W. - Rank in First Lieutenant. Rank out First Lieutenant.

Rhodes, Caleb - Rank in Private. Rank out Private.

Rhodes, Joseph - Rank in Private. Rank out Private.

Rhyne, Adam A. - Rank in Captain. Rank out Captain.

Rhyne, Jacob H. - Rank in Private. Rank out Private.

Rhyne, Jacob K. - Rank in Private. Rank out Private.

Roberts, Michael - Rank in Private. Rank out Private.

Rohm, David - Rank in Private. Rank out Private.

Rutledge, Robert - Rank in Private. Rank out Private.

Sanders, Simpson - Rank in Private. Rank out Private.

Shrum, Michael - Rank in Private. Rank out Private.

Smith, Andrew - Rank in Private. Rank out Private.

Smith, Elijah - Rank in Private. Rank out Private.

Smith, Henry - Rank in Private. Rank out Private.

Stone, John - Rank in Private. Rank out Private.

Stroup, J.E. - Rank in Private. Rank out Private.

Summerville, Robert J. - Rank in Private. Rank out Private.

Thornburg, Daniel - Rank in Private. Rank out Private.

Thornburg, William - Rank in Private. Rank out Private.

Tiege, William - Rank in Private. Rank out Private.

Whitesides, Edward - Rank in Private. Rank out Private.

Company F

Shinn, John L. - Rank in First Lieutenant. Rank out Captain.

Smith, Paul B. C. - Rank in Captain. Rank out Captain.

Morrison, Robert H. - Rank in Second Lieutenant. Rank out First Lieutenant.

Ochler, George F. - Rank in Private. Rank out Second Lieutenant.

Elkins, Willis - Rank in Second Lieutenant. Rank out Second Lieutenant.

Alexander, A. C. - Rank in Private. Rank out Private.

Banker, William L. - Rank in Private. Rank out Private.

Barringer, George W. - Rank in Private. Rank out Private.

Barringer, John - Rank in Private. Rank out Private.

Barringer, Martin - Rank in Private. Rank out Private.

Bast, E.W. - Rank in Private. Rank out Private.

Bast, Hiram - Rank in Private. Rank out Private.

Benson, J. S. - Rank in Private. Rank out Private.

Blackwelder, Alex - Rank in Private. Rank out Private.

Boger, Allen - Rank in Private. Rank out Private.

Brumley, W. R. - Rank in Private. Rank out Private.

Caldwell, D. S. - Rank in Private. Rank out Private.

Caldwell, Daniel S. - Rank in Private. Rank out Private.

Carrigan, W.F. - Rank in Private. Rank out Private.

Cline, Edmund - Rank in Private. Rank out Private.

Cook, Joseph - Rank in Private. Rank out Private.

Cox, Peter - Rank in Private. Rank out Private.

Cress, Moses - Rank in Private. Rank out Private.

Darton, C.L. - Rank in Private. Rank out Private.

Degarmatt, C. H. - Rank in Private. Rank out Private.

Dejurnatt, C. H. - Rank in Private. Rank out Private.

Eagle, Daniel - Rank in Private. Rank out Private.

Ernhart, J.A. - Rank in Private. Rank out Private.

Fox, A. - Rank in Private. Rank out Private.

Garman, Michael - Rank in Private. Rank out Private.

Gilliam, W. M. - Rank in Private. Rank out Private.

Gillian, W. M. - Rank in Private. Rank out Private.

Goodman, H. C. - Rank in Private. Rank out Private.

Goodnight, Isaac - Rank in Private. Rank out Private.

Goodnight, W. G. - Rank in Private. Rank out Private.

Green, George W. - Rank in Private. Rank out Private.

Harkey, Martin - Rank in Private. Rank out Private.

Harris, McAney - Rank in Private. Rank out Private.

Hileman, John - Rank in Private. Rank out Private.

Insenhour, J.A. - Rank in Private. Rank out Private.

Kiser, Erwin - Rank in Private. Rank out Private.

Lefler, Thomas - Rank in Private. Rank out Private.

Leutz, P. J. - Rank in Private. Rank out Private.

Linn, John - Rank in Private. Rank out Private.

Martin, E. L. - Rank in Private. Rank out Private.

Martin, E. R. - Rank in Private. Rank out Private.

Mass, Edward - Rank in Private. Rank out Private.

McKibbon, A. J. - Rank in Private. Rank out Private.

McKibbon, R. L. - Rank in Private. Rank out Private.

McLelland, James C. - Rank in Private. Rank out Private.

Melchor, Daniel - Rank in Private. Rank out Private.

Miller, Paul - Rank in Private. Rank out Private.

Moose, John - Rank in Private. Rank out Private.

Morrison, Pinkney - Rank in Private. Rank out Private.

Myers, Daniel - Rank in Private. Rank out Private.

Nusman, Sol - Rank in Private. Rank out Private.

Ockler, George F. - Rank in Private. Rank out Private.

Overcash, J. - Rank in Private. Rank out Private.

Parham, H. C. - Rank in Private. Rank out Private.

Parrish, David L. - Rank in Private. Rank out Private.

Phillips, Harvey - Rank in Private. Rank out Private.

Propst, George A. - Rank in Private. Rank out Private.

Reed, John L. - Rank in Private. Rank out Private.

Ridenhour, E.N. - Rank in Private. Rank out Private.

Rinehart, Matthias - Rank in Private. Rank out Private.

Rinehart, Paul - Rank in Private. Rank out Private.

Rogers, S. K. - Rank in Private. Rank out Private.

Rogers, W. P. - Rank in Private. Rank out Private.

Sossaman, John C. - Rank in Private. Rank out Private.

Stirewalt, Jacob - Rank in Private. Rank out Private.

Stisewalt, Paul - Rank in Private. Rank out Private.

Stowe, Henry M. - Rank in Private. Rank out Private.

Stowe, Levi - Rank in Private. Rank out Private.

Suther, A.M. - Rank in Private. Rank out Private.

Traulman, Peter - Rank in Private. Rank out Private.

Tucker, Darling - Rank in Private. Rank out Private.

Tucker, John F. - Rank in Private. Rank out Private.

Urey, Levi - Rank in Private. Rank out Private.

Wafford, John - Rank in Private. Rank out Private.

Wagoner, John - Rank in Private. Rank out Private.

Wallace, M.A. - Rank in Private. Rank out Private.

Walter, A. - Rank in Private. Rank out Private.

Weaver, Esau - Rank in Private. Rank out Private.

Weaver, Esrom - Rank in Private. Rank out Private.

Winecoff, Daniel - Rank in Private. Rank out Private.

Winecoff, Henry - Rank in Private. Rank out Private.

Winecoff, Vol - Rank in Private. Rank out Private.

Woods, T.L. - Rank in Private. Rank out Private.

Yost, Aaron - Rank in Private. Rank out Private.

Company G

Alexander, Ira - Rank in Private. Rank out Private.

Alexander, Lee - Rank in Private. Rank out Private.

Alexander, M. J. - Rank in Private. Rank out Private.

Alexander, N. - Rank in Private. Rank out Private.

Allen, Albert - Rank in Private. Rank out Private.

Allison, I. A. - Rank in Private. Rank out Private.

Archer, Wilson - Rank in Private. Rank out Private.

Asbury, Daniel - Rank in Private. Rank out Private.

Bailey, J. R. - Rank in Private. Rank out Private.

Baker, C. M. - Rank in Private. Rank out Private.

Banker, J. L. - Rank in Private. Rank out Private.

Barnhill, S.H. - Rank in Private. Rank out Private.

Bartlett, James - Rank in Private. Rank out Private.

Black, W. N. - Rank in Private. Rank out Private.

Blackwood, J. J. - Rank in Private. Rank out Private.

Blakeley, Hugh - Rank in Private. Rank out Private.

Blakely, U - Rank in Private. Rank out Private.

Blakley, Hugh - Rank in Private. Rank out Private.

Boyce, S. A. - Rank in Private. Rank out Private.

Burns, J. W. - Rank in Private. Rank out Private.

Capps, Joseph - Rank in Private. Rank out Private.

Carr, C.M. - Rank in Private. Rank out Private.

Carroll, William - Rank in Private. Rank out Private.

Carter, William - Rank in Private. Rank out Private.

Caruthers, J.K. - Rank in Private. Rank out Private.

Cassiom, Burwell - Rank in Private. Rank out Private.

Cassiom, William - Rank in Private. Rank out Private.

Cochren, E.P. - Rank in Sergeant. Rank out Sergeant.

Coffee, H.S. - Rank in Private. Rank out Private.

Davis, J. M. - Rank in Corporal. Rank out Corporal.

Davis, Joseph - Rank in Private. Rank out Private.

Dennis, J. C. - Rank in Private. Rank out Private.

Dennis, Philaman - Rank in Private. Rank out Private.

Dennis, William - Rank in Private. Rank out Private.

Dulin, Ambrose - Rank in Private. Rank out Private.

Dulin, J.J. - Rank in Private. Rank out Private.

Dulin, W.L. - Rank in Private. Rank out Private.

Dunn, D.F. - Rank in Private. Rank out Private.

Dunn, David F. - Rank in Private. Rank out Private.

Elliott, J.B. - Rank in Private. Rank out Private.

Ewart, H.D. - Rank in Private. Rank out Private.

Farris, S. J. - Rank in Private. Rank out Private.

Ferris, S. J. - Rank in Private. Rank out Private.

Fite, G. S. - Rank in Private. Rank out Private.

Flow, E. W. - Rank in Private. Rank out Private.

Frazier, Charles - Rank in Private. Rank out Private.

Galloway, F.L. - Rank in Private. Rank out Private.

Gamble, John - Rank in Private. Rank out Private.

Garrison, Samuel - Rank in Senior Second Lieutenant. Rank out Second Lieutenant.

Griffin, Solomon - Rank in Private. Rank out Private.

Griffith, A. H. - Rank in Private. Rank out Private.

Hannon, T.A. - Rank in Private. Rank out Private.

Harkey, Richard - Rank in Private. Rank out Private.

Hawston, W. L. - Rank in Corporal. Rank out Corporal.

Helms, Hugh - Rank in Private. Rank out Private.

Hobbs, John - Rank in Private. Rank out Private.

Hodges, P. A. - Rank in Private. Rank out Private.

Hood, J.C. - Rank in Private. Rank out Private.

Hoover, H. - Rank in Private. Rank out Private.

Houston, W.L. - Rank in Private. Rank out Private.

Hucks, S.A. - Rank in Private. Rank out Private.

Hunter, John - Rank in Private. Rank out Private.

Hunter, R.B. - Rank in Sergeant. Rank out Sergeant.

Johnson, J.H. - Rank in Private. Rank out Private.

Johnson, J.L. - Rank in Private. Rank out Private.

Johnson, William A. - Rank in Private. Rank out Private.

Jordan, George - Rank in Private. Rank out Private.

Judden, George - Rank in Private. Rank out Private.

Kirk, John - Rank in Private. Rank out Private.

Lawing, Joseph - Rank in Private. Rank out Private.

Lawing, Thomas - Rank in Private. Rank out Private.

McCall, J. A. - Rank in Private. Rank out Private.

McCorkle, William H. - Rank in Private. Rank out Private.

McCraney, J. M. - Rank in Private. Rank out Private.

McGinis, E. P. - Rank in Sergeant. Rank out Sergeant.

McIntosh, A. - Rank in Private. Rank out Private.

McKinney, Wesley - Rank in Private. Rank out Private.

McKnight, John M. - Rank in Private. Rank out Private.

McNeely, Robert A. - Rank in Captain. Rank out Captain.

Moore, Alexander - Rank in Private. Rank out Private.

Morrow, J. A. - Rank in Private. Rank out Private.

Neely, John S. - Rank in Junior Second Lieutenant. Rank out Second Lieutenant.

Noles, W. P. - Rank in Private. Rank out Private.

Nothey, James - Rank in Private. Rank out Private.

Ochler, John - Rank in Private. Rank out Private.

Oglesby, S. - Rank in Private. Rank out Private.

Pahel, John - Rank in Private. Rank out Private.

Pendergrass, Jesse - Rank in Private. Rank out Private.

Porter, J. L. - Rank in First Sergeant/Ordnance Sergeant. Rank out First Sergeant/Ordnance Sergeant.

Rea, John K. - Rank in Private. Rank out Private.

Rea, Lee - Rank in Private. Rank out Private.

Reid, J. Y. - Rank in Private. Rank out Private.

Reid, John - Rank in Private. Rank out Private.

Roberts, J. M. - Rank in Private. Rank out Private.

Robinson, Elam - Rank in Private. Rank out Private.

Robinson, Harvey - Rank in Private. Rank out Private.

Ross, J. C. - Rank in Private. Rank out Private.

Rudasil, Jonas - Rank in Private. Rank out Private.

Saunders, Jesse - Rank in Private. Rank out Private.

Sharp, James - Rank in Private. Rank out Private.

Shipping, Moses - Rank in Corporal. Rank out Corporal.

Shuping, Moses - Rank in Corporal. Rank out Corporal.

Simerel, T. J. - Rank in Second Sergeant. Rank out Second Sergeant.

Simpson, Jefferson - Rank in Private. Rank out Private.

Smith, Ed - Rank in Private. Rank out Private.

Soserman, William - Rank in Private. Rank out Private.

Springs, E. A. - Rank in Corporal. Rank out Corporal.

Springs, J. M. - Rank in Private. Rank out Private.

Stanferd, M. P. - Rank in Private. Rank out Private.

Stewart, A. A. - Rank in Private. Rank out Private.

Stewart, William - Rank in Private. Rank out Private.

Strong, John M. - Rank in First Lieutenant. Rank out Surgeon.

Underwood, Willis - Rank in Private. Rank out Private.

Walice, James - Rank in Corporal. Rank out Corporal.

Wallace, John N. - Rank in Private. Rank out Private.

Watt, Eron - Rank in Private. Rank out Private.

Weddington, R. H. - Rank in Private. Rank out Private.

Whitesides, S. M. - Rank in Private. Rank out Private.

Wilson, S. S. - Rank in Private. Rank out Private.

Wolfe, J. H. - Rank in Private. Rank out Private.

Company H

Beam, Martin - Rank in Private. Rank out Private.

Beason, Robert - Rank in Private. Rank out Private.

Bigham, Christopher - Rank in Private. Rank out Private.

Blackwood, J. L. - Rank in Private. Rank out Private.

Blandon, Francis A. - Rank in Private. Rank out Private.

Blanton, E. A. - Rank in Private. Rank out Private.

Borders, Henderson - Rank in Private. Rank out Private.

Bradshaw, Seth - Rank in Private. Rank out Private.

Bridges, A. S. - Rank in Private. Rank out Private.

Bridges, Washington - Rank in Private. Rank out Private.

Caudry, John - Rank in Private. Rank out Private.

Chambers, E.S. - Rank in Private. Rank out Private.

Chandler, Melchisedic - Rank in Third Lieutenant. Rank out Second Lieutenant.

Crotts, John - Rank in Private. Rank out Private.

Daly, Jesse - Rank in Private. Rank out Private.

Davidson, Jesse - Rank in Private. Rank out Private.

Davidson, W. B. - Rank in Private. Rank out Private.

Davis, B. P. - Rank in Private. Rank out Private.

Doty, Jesse - Rank in Private. Rank out Private.

Effler, George - Rank in Private. Rank out Private.

Etters, Samuel - Rank in Private. Rank out Private.

Falls, A. U. - Rank in Private. Rank out Private.

Franeberger, William - Rank in Private. Rank out Private.

Gilham, C.W. - Rank in Private. Rank out Private.

Goforth, Andrew - Rank in Private. Rank out Private.

Graves, Thomas - Rank in Private. Rank out Private.

Green, M. H. - Rank in Private. Rank out Private.

Grigg, W. J. - Rank in Private. Rank out Private.

Ham, John - Rank in Private. Rank out Private.

Hardin, Jesse - Rank in Private. Rank out Private.

Harmon, John G. - Rank in Lieutenant. Rank out Lieutenant.

Hendrick, James - Rank in Private. Rank out Private.

Howell, J.P. - Rank in Private. Rank out Private.

Howell, T.W. - Rank in Private. Rank out Private.

Hoyle, Henry - Rank in Private. Rank out Private.

Hughes, James - Rank in Private. Rank out Private.

Hull, Benjamin - Rank in Private. Rank out Private.

Hull, David - Rank in Private. Rank out Private.

Hullett, John - Rank in Private. Rank out Private.

Humphries, J.L. - Rank in Private. Rank out Private.

Humphries, Lawson - Rank in Private. Rank out Private.

Humphries, Oliver - Rank in Private. Rank out Private.

Hunt, Joseph - Rank in Private. Rank out Private.

Jones, I. J. - Rank in Private. Rank out Private.

Justice, Benjamin - Rank in Private. Rank out Private.

Justice, John - Rank in Private. Rank out Private.

Kendrick, Thomas - Rank in Private. Rank out Private.

Ladford, C.E. - Rank in Private. Rank out Private.

Ladford, J.R. - Rank in Private. Rank out Private.

Lovelace, Asa - Rank in Private. Rank out Private.

Lucas, Peter - Rank in Private. Rank out Private.

Magness, Robert - Rank in Captain. Rank out Captain.

Martin, Andrew - Rank in Private. Rank out Private.

McCraw, Robert - Rank in Private. Rank out Private.

McDaniel, William - Rank in Private. Rank out Private.

McEntire, William - Rank in Private. Rank out Private.

McKiney, James - Rank in Private. Rank out Private.

McSwain, H. K. - Rank in Private. Rank out Private.

McSwain, W. B. - Rank in Private. Rank out Private.

Mooney, Daniel - Rank in Private. Rank out Private.

Mooney, David - Rank in Private. Rank out Private.

Moorehead, E. J. - Rank in Private. Rank out Private.

Morrison, D. J. - Rank in Private. Rank out Private.

Moss, Edward - Rank in Private. Rank out Private.

Moss, Martin - Rank in Private. Rank out Private.

Patterson, F. A. - Rank in Private. Rank out Private.

Patterson, J. M. - Rank in Private. Rank out Private.

Peeler, J. H. - Rank in Private. Rank out Private.

Price, Ransom - Rank in Second Lieutenant. Rank out Second Lieutenant.

Price, Robert - Rank in Second Lieutenant. Rank out Second Lieutenant.

Quinn, Martin - Rank in Private. Rank out Private.

Rippy, James - Rank in Private. Rank out Private.

Roark, R.M. - Rank in Private. Rank out Private.

Ross, Mathew - Rank in Private. Rank out Private.

Smith, Thomas - Rank in Private. Rank out Private.

Sparks, Alpheus - Rank in Private. Rank out Private.

Sullivan, J.W. - Rank in Private. Rank out Private.

Tate, Asa - Rank in Private. Rank out Private.

Tucker, J.B. - Rank in Private. Rank out Private.

Turner, R.B. - Rank in Private. Rank out Private.

Turner, Wiley - Rank in Private. Rank out Private.

Wallis, David - Rank in Private. Rank out Private.

Wallis, J.Y. - Rank in Private. Rank out Private.

Ware, A.B. - Rank in Private. Rank out Private.

Whitt, J. W. - Rank in Private. Rank out Private.

Wiley, J. R. - Rank in Private. Rank out Private.

Wood, H. S. - Rank in Private. Rank out Private.

Wood, T. W. - Rank in Private. Rank out Private.

Wright, Nathan - Rank in Private. Rank out Private.

Company I

Austin, Josiah - Rank in First Lieutenant. Rank out First Lieutenant.

Bass, D.H. - Rank in Private. Rank out Private.

Beck, A. W. - Rank in Private. Rank out Private.

Bevins, James - Rank in Private. Rank out Private.

Borr, R. K. - Rank in Private. Rank out Private.

Boyt, W. R. W. - Rank in Private. Rank out Private.

Brewer, Sal R. - Rank in Private. Rank out Private.

Broom, Thomas - Rank in Private. Rank out Private.

Broom, W. W. - Rank in Private. Rank out Private.

Bussey, Henry - Rank in Private. Rank out Private.

Carpenter, Isaac - Rank in Private. Rank out Private.

Cason, J.F. - Rank in Private. Rank out Private.

Chandy, Allen - Rank in Private. Rank out Private.

Corelock, W.J. - Rank in Private. Rank out Private.

Cowlee, C.B. - Rank in Private. Rank out Private.

Daste, James M. - Rank in Private. Rank out Private.

Dees, Christopher - Rank in Private. Rank out Private.

Dothe(r), J.M. - Rank in Private. Rank out .

Eller, David - Rank in Private. Rank out Private.

Freeman, Henderson - Rank in Private. Rank out Private.

Griffin, James C. - Rank in Private. Rank out Private.

Harkness, Elias - Rank in Private. Rank out Private.

Hartsell, Aaron - Rank in Private. Rank out Private.

Heinby, Eli - Rank in Private. Rank out Private.

Helms, Daniel - Rank in Private. Rank out Private.

Helms, Henderson - Rank in Private. Rank out Private.

Helms, Hiliard - Rank in Private. Rank out Private.

Helms, Isaac - Rank in Private. Rank out Private.

Helms, Lee - Rank in Private. Rank out Private.

Helms, Washington - Rank in Private. Rank out Private.

Helms, William - Rank in Private. Rank out Private.

Horton, B.G. - Rank in Private. Rank out Private.

Houston, James - Rank in Private. Rank out Private.

Kisiah, Thomas - Rank in Private. Rank out Private.

Laney, Neb O. - Rank in Private. Rank out Private.

Lemmond, M.M. - Rank in Private. Rank out Private.

Liles, David H. - Rank in Private. Rank out Private.

Long, Adam - Rank in Private. Rank out Private.

Long, G. A. - Rank in Private. Rank out Private.

Long, Jacob - Rank in Private. Rank out Private.

McCall, Sylvester - Rank in Private. Rank out Private.

Meggs, Jonathan - Rank in Private. Rank out Private.

Merill, David - Rank in Private. Rank out Private.

Miller, George - Rank in Private. Rank out Private.

Moore, James - Rank in Private. Rank out Private.

Mulls, Calvin - Rank in Private. Rank out Private.

Parker, William - Rank in Private. Rank out Private.

Pheifer, A. J. - Rank in Private. Rank out Private.

Pheifer, Elisha - Rank in Private. Rank out Private.

Pheifer, John E. - Rank in Private. Rank out Private.

Phillips, Robert - Rank in Private. Rank out Private.

Porter, J. N. - Rank in Private. Rank out Private.

Presley, Eli - Rank in Private. Rank out Private.

Privett, Martin - Rank in Private. Rank out Private.

Ramsey, W. R. - Rank in Private. Rank out Private.

Rice, Stewart - Rank in Private. Rank out Private.

Richardson, J. F. - Rank in Private. Rank out Private.

Richardson, M. J. - Rank in Private. Rank out Private.

Riggins, Charles D. - Rank in Private. Rank out Private.

Roane, L.K. - Rank in Captain. Rank out Captain.

Rogers, Calvin - Rank in Second Lieutenant. Rank out Second Lieutenant.

Rone, Loyd K. - Rank in Captain. Rank out Captain.

Rushing, Green B. - Rank in Private. Rank out Private.

Russell, D. G. - Rank in Private. Rank out Private.

Secrest, Samuel T. - Rank in Second Lieutenant. Rank out Second Lieutenant.

Simpson, David - Rank in Private. Rank out Private.

Simpson, Jackson - Rank in Private. Rank out Private.

Sinclair, D. A. - Rank in Private. Rank out Private.

Smith, J. E. W. - Rank in Private. Rank out Private.

Stigall, A. B. - Rank in Private. Rank out Private.

Stigall, J. B. - Rank in Private. Rank out Private.

Strickland, John - Rank in Private. Rank out Private.

Swanner, J.M. - Rank in Private. Rank out Private.

Thompson, S.T. - Rank in Private. Rank out Private.

Tomberlin, Durias - Rank in Private. Rank out Private.

Yandell, Sherwood - Rank in Private. Rank out Private.

Yorborough, G. W. M. - Rank in Private. Rank out Private.

Company K

Alexander, N. A. - Rank in Private. Rank out Private.

Ballard, John - Rank in Private. Rank out Private.

Ballard, John F. - Rank in Private. Rank out Private.

Ballard, William - Rank in Private. Rank out Private.

Bigham, W. C. - Rank in Private. Rank out Private.

Black, J. - Rank in Private. Rank out Private.

Boyles, Josiah - Rank in Private. Rank out Private.

Brotherton, William - Rank in Private. Rank out Private.

Bynum, J. T. - Rank in Private. Rank out Private.

Carpenter, Solomon - Rank in Private. Rank out Private.

Childers, Alfred - Rank in Private. Rank out Private.

Cornwell, James M. - Rank in Private. Rank out Private.

Crouse, John - Rank in Private. Rank out Private.

Dellinger, Daniel H. - Rank in Private. Rank out Private.

Dellinger, John F. - Rank in Private. Rank out Private.

Dunn, L.F. - Rank in Private. Rank out Private.

Farris, S. J. - Rank in Private. Rank out Private.

Feaster, J. C. C. - Rank in Private. Rank out Sergeant Major.

Ferris, S. J. - Rank in Private. Rank out Private.

Fester, J. C. C. - Rank in Private. Rank out Sergeant Major.

Finch, John - Rank in Private. Rank out Private.

Foaster, J. C. C. - Rank in Private. Rank out Sergeant Major.

Goodson, Alexander - Rank in Private. Rank out Private.

Goodson, J. - Rank in Private. Rank out Private.

Hefner, Stephen - Rank in Private. Rank out Private.

Hill, John F. - Rank in Captain. Rank out Captain.

Hinson, William - Rank in Private. Rank out Private.

Hoke, Alfred L. - Rank in Second Lieutenant. Rank out Second Lieutenant.

Hoke, Lewis A. - Rank in Second Lieutenant. Rank out Second Lieutenant.

Hoofner, David - Rank in Private. Rank out Private.

Hoover, H. - Rank in Private. Rank out Private.

Hoover, L.S. - Rank in Private. Rank out Private.

Houser, Isaac - Rank in Private. Rank out Private.

Huss, Jacob - Rank in Private. Rank out Private.

Johnson, A.R. - Rank in Private. Rank out Private.

Jonas, John - Rank in Private. Rank out Private.

Kanipe, Adam - Rank in Private. Rank out Private.

Kanipe, David - Rank in Private. Rank out Private.

Kanipe, Joseph - Rank in Private. Rank out Private.

Keener, Lewis - Rank in Private. Rank out Private.

Kelley, A. J. - Rank in Private. Rank out Private.

King, J.H. - Rank in Private. Rank out Private.

Kistler, Phillip - Rank in Private. Rank out Private.

Lackey, John - Rank in Private. Rank out Private.

Lawing, Thomas - Rank in Private. Rank out Private.

Leonhardt, Lawrance - Rank in Private. Rank out Private.

Lore, Ephraim - Rank in Private. Rank out Private.

Love, Ephraim - Rank in Private. Rank out Private.

Lynn, Archibald - Rank in Private. Rank out Private.

Marshall, William - Rank in Private. Rank out Private.

McKnight, John M. - Rank in Private. Rank out Private.

Noles, David - Rank in Private. Rank out Private.

Noles, W. R. - Rank in Private. Rank out Private.

Patterson, R. M. - Rank in Private. Rank out Private.

Paysbur, J. W. - Rank in Private. Rank out Private.

Petry, Lawson - Rank in Private. Rank out Private.

Porter, James M. - Rank in Private. Rank out Private.

Proctor, Richard - Rank in First Lieutenant. Rank out First Lieutenant.

Proptr, Michael - Rank in Private. Rank out Private.

Ramsur, D. W. - Rank in Private. Rank out Private.

Reep, Daniel - Rank in Private. Rank out Private.

Reid, J. Y. - Rank in Private. Rank out Private.

Robertson, Andrew - Rank in Private. Rank out Private.

Robinson, Elam - Rank in Private. Rank out Private.

Rouk, Jesse - Rank in Private. Rank out Private.

Ruffield, George - Rank in Private. Rank out Private.

Sain, Jacob - Rank in Private. Rank out Private.

Settine, Emanuel - Rank in Private. Rank out Private.

Sherrill, James - Rank in Private. Rank out Private.

Shronce, S.R. - Rank in Private. Rank out Private.

Smith, Martin - Rank in Private. Rank out Private.

Sneed, James - Rank in Private. Rank out Private.

Sowrey, Adam - Rank in Private. Rank out Private.

Spake, Sam - Rank in Private. Rank out Private.

Springs, Alexander - Rank in Private. Rank out Private.

Stewart, Archibald - Rank in Third Lieutenant. Rank out Second Lieutenant.

Underwood, Willis - Rank in Private. Rank out Private.

Wilburn, H. D. A. - Rank in Private. Rank out Private.

Wilson, Maxwell - Rank in Private. Rank out Private.

Company L

Salmon, Elisha - Rank in Private. Rank out .

Company Unknown

Campbell, George W. - Rank in Private. Rank out Private.

Lofton, Joel - Rank in Private. Rank out Private.

Bibliography

Clark, Walter, ed. Histories of the Several Regiments and Battalions from North Carolina in the Great War, l86l-'65... Vol. 4. Cartersville, GA: Eastern Digital Resources, 1998. E573.4H57.1982v4. (Unit history and roster of officers).

Crute, Joseph H., Jr. Units of the Confederate States Army. Midlothian, VA: Derwent Books, 1987. Ref. Concise summary of the unit's service.

Hill, Gen. D. H. Confederate Military History Vol. IV Cartersville, GA: Eastern Digital Resources, 1999. 823 pps. REF: History of the Civil War in North Carolina. Numerous mentions of the unit and biographical sketches of the officers. CD-ROM available.

Howard, Oliver Otis. Letters. Howard Collection. Bowdoin College Library, Brunswick, Maine.

Manarin, Louis H. comp. North Carolina Troops, 1861-1865: A Roster. Vol. 1. Raleigh, NC: Office of Arch & Hist, 1966. E573.3M3v1. Brief history of the unit. Subsequent pages contain a unit roster.

Moore, John W. Roster of North Carolina Troops in the War Between the States. Vol. 4. Raleigh, NC: Ashe & Gatling, 1882. Cartersville, GA: Eastern Digital Resources, 1998E573.3N87v4. (Unit roster).

Osborn, Thomas Ward.. "Autiobiographical Sketch." Florida State University, Tallahassee.

Rigdon, John C. <u>66 Days of Hell</u> Cartersville, GA: Eastern Digital Resources, 1998

Rigdon, John C. <u>Historical Sketch & Roster of the North Carolina 4th Infantry Regiment Senior Reserves</u> Cartersville, GA: Eastern Digital Resources, 1998

Rigdon, John C. <u>The Battle of Aiken</u>. Cartersville, GA: Eastern Digital Resources, 1998

Sherman, William Tecumseh. "Report of Major General William T. Sherman to the Hon. Committee on the Conduct of the War. 2 vols. Washington, D.C. Government Printing Office. 1866.

Sifakis, Stewart. <u>Compendium of the Confederate Armies: North Carolina.</u> NY: Facts on File, 1992. E573S53.1992. (Unit organizational history).

Newspapers and Articles:

Gibbes, James E. Philadelphia Times (Sept. 20, 1880)

Hesseltine, William B. and Larry Gara, eds. "Sherman Burns the Libraries", South Carolina Historical Magazine IV no. 3 (July 1954)

On Line Sites:

http://members.aol.com/jweaver301/nc/5ncsrres.htm

http://www.ssvawebs.com/townkenbridge/history.htm

http://www.ci.salisbury.nc.us/prison/csprison3.htm

Index

Bradshaw, Seth ~ Co. H
Brady, R. A. ~ Co. D
Brandon, N. H. ~ Co. D
Brawley, J. G. ~ Co. D
Brawley, John M. ~ Co. B
Brawley, N. S. ~ Co. D
Brewer, Sal R. ~ Co. I
Bridges, A. S. ~ Co. H
Bridges, Washington ~ Co. H
Broom, Thomas ~ Co. I
Broom, W. W. ~ Co. I
Brotherton, William ~ Co. K
Brown, A. ~ Co. D
Brown, John D. ~ Co. B
Brown, Philip W. ~ Co. E
Brown, T. A. ~ Co. D
Brown, William M. ~ Co. B
Brumley, W. R. ~ Co. F
Bumgarner, Aman ~ Co. C
Burch, T. F. ~ Co. C
Burke, Monroe ~ Co. E
Burns, J. W. ~ Co. G
Burress, Ezekiel ~ Co. C
Bussey, Henry ~ Co. I
Bynum, J. T. ~ Co. K
Caldwell, Daniel S. ~ Co. F
Calvert, R. S. ~ Co. D
Campbell, George W. ~ Co. Unknown
Campbell, T. M. ~ Co. D
Capps, Joseph ~ Co. G
Carpenter, Abel ~ Co. E
Carpenter, Alfred ~ Co. E
Carpenter, Isaac ~ Co. I
Carpenter, John ~ Co. C
Carpenter, Solomon ~ Co. K
Carpenter, W.B. ~ Co. E
Carr, Charles M. ~ Co. D
Carrigan, W.F. ~ Co. F
Carroll, William ~ Co. G
Carter, N. ~ Co. D
Carter, William ~ Co. G
Caruthers, J.K. ~ Co. G
Cason, J.F. ~ Co. I

Casper, David ~ Co. B
Casper, Levi ~ Co. B
Cassiom, Burwell ~ Co. G
Cassiom, William ~ Co. G
Cauble, Isaac ~ Co. B
Caudry, John ~ Co. H
Caulter, Eli S. ~ Co. C
Chambers, E.S. ~ Co. H
Chandler, Melchisedic ~ Co. H
Chandy, Allen ~ Co. I
Chaplin, Solomon ~ Co. A
Childers, Alfred ~ Co. K
Christian, George W. ~ Co. D
Christie, John A. ~ Co. B
Claninger, John ~ Co. C
Clemmer, Adam ~ Co. E
Click, J.G. ~ Co. D
Clifford, James ~ Co. A
Clifford, John W. ~ Co. A
Cline, Aman ~ Co. C
Cline, Edmund ~ Co. F
Clinton, DeWitt ~ Co. A
Clodfelter, George A. ~ Co. B
Clodfelter, John F. ~ Co. B
Cochren, E.P. ~ Co. G
Coffee, H.S. ~ Co. G
Coleman, John M. ~ Co. B
Collins, Henry ~ Co. D
Condy, William F. ~ Co. D
Cook, Johnson ~ Co. C
Cook, Joseph ~ Co. F
Coon, George ~ Co. B
Coons, John ~ Co. C
Corelock, W.J. ~ Co. I
Cornwell, James M. ~ Co. K
Correll, Levi ~ Co. B
Costner, Joseph ~ Co. E
Cowlee, C.B. ~ Co. I
Cox, Patrick ~ Co. E
Cox, Peter ~ Co. F
Cozart, Hiram W. ~ Co. B
Cranfill, Alex ~ Co. A
Crawford, W.R. ~ Co. D

Crawly, Jackson ~ Co. A
Cress, Moses ~ Co. F
Cristy, John A. ~ Co. B
Crotts, John ~ Co. H
Crouse, John ~ Co. K
Cruse, Charles A. ~ Co. B
Cruse, G.B. ~ Co. D
Current, A. ~ Co. D
Daly, Jesse ~ Co. H
Dancey, Enos ~ Co. D
Danner, Alexander ~ Co. C
Darton, C.L. ~ Co. F
Daste, James M. ~ Co. I
Davidson, Jesse ~ Co. H
Davidson, W. B. ~ Co. H
Davis, B. P. ~ Co. H
Davis, George C. ~ Co. A
Davis, J. M. ~ Co. G
Davis, James L. ~ Co. C
Davis, Joseph ~ Co. G
Daywalt, William ~ Co. D
Deal, Franklina ~ Co. C
Deal, John ~ Co. B
Deal, L. A. ~ Co. C
Dees, Christopher ~ Co. I
Degarmatt, C. H. ~ Co. F
Deitz, Caleb ~ Co. C
Deitz, Lazarus ~ Co. C
Dejurnatt, C. H. ~ Co. F
Dellinger, Daniel H. ~ Co. K
Dellinger, John F. ~ Co. K
Dennis, J. C. ~ Co. G
Dennis, Philaman ~ Co. G
Dennis, William ~ Co. G
Dillen, William ~ Co. E
Dishman, William ~ Co. D
Dothe(r), J.M. ~ Co. I
Doty, Jesse ~ Co. H
Douherty, David ~ Co. B
Downs, William R. ~ Co. A
Drake, Green ~ Co. A
Dulin, Ambrose ~ Co. G
Dulin, J.J. ~ Co. G

Dulin, W.L. ~ Co. G
Dunkan, Harvey ~ Co. D
Dunn, David F. ~ Co. G
Dunn, L.F. ~ Co. K
Dyson, Tilmon ~ Co. A
Dyson, William ~ Co. A
Eagh, G.A. ~ Co. D
Eagle, Daniel ~ Co. F
Eagle, David ~ Co. B
Eaton, B.H. ~ Co. A
Eckler, Almon ~ Co. B
Edwards, J.W. ~ Co. D
Edwards, John ~ Co. C
Edwards, Sparhart ~ Co. C
Effler, George ~ Co. H
Elkins, Willis ~ Co. F
Eller, David ~ Co. I
Eller, Michael ~ Co. B
Elliott, J.B. ~ Co. G
Ellis, Willis ~ Co. B
Ernhart, J.A. ~ Co. F
Ernheart, Henry ~ Co. B
Ervwin, Adolphus ~ Co. D
Ervwin, J.H. ~ Co. D
Estes, Irvin ~ Co. B
Etters, Samuel ~ Co. H
Ewart, H.D. ~ Co. G
Faircloth, Thomas ~ Co. A
Falls, A. U. ~ Co. H
Falls, And. J. ~ Co. E
Farris, S. J. ~ Co. G,K
Feaster (Fester / Foaster), J. C. C. ~ Co. K
Ferris, S. J. ~ Co. G,K
File, Tobias ~ Co. B
Finch, John ~ Co. K
Finger, John ~ Co. C
Fisher, Coleman ~ Co. C
Fite, G. S. ~ Co. G
Flow, E. W. ~ Co. G
Fore, James M. ~ Co. E
Fowler, J. W. ~ Co. D
Fox, A. ~ Co. F
Fraley, Thomas D. ~ Co. B

Franeberger, William ~ Co. H
Frazier, Alex ~ Co. C
Frazier, Charles ~ Co. G
Freeland, Thomas A. ~ Co. D
Freeman, Henderson ~ Co. I
Freeze, John L. ~ Co. B
Freis, Daniel ~ Co. D
Fromberger, Ambrose ~ Co. E
Fry, Hannon ~ Co. A
Fry, Salaman ~ Co. C
Fullbright, David ~ Co. C
Fullbright, Henry ~ Co. C
Gaither, J.J. ~ Co. D
Gaither, Martin ~ Co. D
Galloway, F.L. ~ Co. G
Gamble, John ~ Co. G
Gant, A.J. ~ Co. E*
Garawood, Nathaniel ~ Co. A
Garman, Michael ~ Co. F
Garrison, Samuel ~ Co. G
Gaston, Robert H. ~ Co. E
Gibson, Felix ~ Co. D
Gibson, Fishling ~ Co. D
Gilham, C.W. ~ Co. H
Gilliam (Gillian), W. M. ~ Co. F
Glasscock, Thomas N. B. ~ Co. A
Glenn, Stanhope ~ Co. E
Goforth, Andrew ~ Co. H
Goforth, Thomas B. ~ Co. D
Goodman, George ~ Co. B
Goodman, H. C. ~ Co. F
Goodnight, Isaac ~ Co. F
Goodnight, W. G. ~ Co. F
Goodson, Alexander ~ Co. K
Goodson, J. ~ Co. K
Graham, William ~ Co. B
Grant, John ~ Co. D
Graves, Thomas ~ Co. H
Graves, Wilson ~ Co. A
Gray, H. M. ~ Co. D
Green, George W. ~ Co. F
Green, M. H. ~ Co. H
Gregory, M. ~ Co. D

Griffin, James C. ~ Co. I
Griffin, Solomon ~ Co. G
Griffith, A. H. ~ Co. G
Grigg, W. J. ~ Co. H
Gross, William ~ Co. D
Gullet, James ~ Co. A
Guthery, N.C.R. ~ Co. D
Guthry, Martin ~ Co. D
Hair, D.J. ~ Co. D
Haire, D.J. ~ Co. D
Haller, Andrew ~ Co. C
Haller, Franklin ~ Co. C
Haller, Peter ~ Co. C
Ham, John ~ Co. H
Hamline, George ~ Co. A
Hampton, F.H. ~ Co. D
Hannon, T.A. ~ Co. G
Hardin, Jesse ~ Co. H
Harkey, George ~ Co. B
Harkey, Martin ~ Co. F
Harkey, Richard ~ Co. G
Harkness, Elias ~ Co. I
Harmon, John G. ~ Co. H
Harris, Henry ~ Co. D
Harris, McAney ~ Co. F
Hartman, James ~ Co. C
Hartsell, Aaron ~ Co. I
Harvey, James N. ~ Co. E
Hauk, Harrison ~ Co. C
Hauser, William H. ~ Co. B
Hawn, Jesse ~ Co. C
Hawn, John ~ Co. C
Hawston, W. L. ~ Co. G
Hayle, H. H. ~ Co. C
Hays, W. ~ Co. D
Heath, Milbourn ~ Co. A
Heathcock, James ~ Co. D
Hefner, Stephen ~ Co. K
Heinby, Eli ~ Co. I
Helms, Daniel ~ Co. I
Helms, Henderson ~ Co. I
Helms, Hiliard ~ Co. I
Helms, Hugh ~ Co. G

Helms, Isaac ~ Co. I
Helms, Lee ~ Co. I
Helms, Washington ~ Co. I
Helms, William ~ Co. I
Helton, L. G. ~ Co. A
Hendrick, James ~ Co. H
Henry, G. H. ~ Co. D
Herman, George ~ Co. C
Hicks, C. P. ~ Co. C
Hileman, John ~ Co. F
Hill, John F. ~ Co. K
Hill, William R. ~ Co. E
Hillard, James ~ Co. A
Hillard, William ~ Co. A
Hinson, William ~ Co. K
Hobbs, H. ~ Co. D
Hobbs, John ~ Co. G
Hodges, P. A. ~ Co. G
Hoffman, David ~ Co. E
Hoffman, Jacob ~ Co. E
Hoke, Alfred L. ~ Co. K
Hoke, John F. ~ Co. F&S
Hoke, Lewis A. ~ Co. K
Holland, Nathaniel ~ Co. D
Holman, Ambrose ~ Co. E
Holman, Jacob ~ Co. E
Holshouser, Jacob ~ Co. B
Holshouser, John ~ Co. B
Homsley, Amos B. ~ Co. E
Hood, J.C. ~ Co. G
Hoofner, David ~ Co. K
Hoover, H. ~ Co. G,K
Hoover, L.S. ~ Co. K
Hoover, Thomas ~ Co. E
Horsley, Richard ~ Co. E
Horton, B.G. ~ Co. I
Horton, Richard ~ Co. E
Horwell, Horace ~ Co. C
Houser, Isaac ~ Co. K
Houser, James ~ Co. A
Houser, James ~ Co. A
Houston, James ~ Co. I
Houston, W.L. ~ Co. G

Howard, David ~ Co. A
Howard, Pinkey ~ Co. D
Howard, William ~ Co. A
Howard, Wilson ~ Co. A
Howell, J.P. ~ Co. H
Howell, T.W. ~ Co. H
Hoyle, Henry ~ Co. H
Hucks, S.A. ~ Co. G
Hudson, H. ~ Co. D
Huffman, Jackson ~ Co. C
Huffman, Martin ~ Co. C
Hughes, James ~ Co. H
Huit, M.M. ~ Co. C
Huithcox, T.A. ~ Co. D
Hull, Benjamin ~ Co. H
Hull, David ~ Co. H
Hullett, John ~ Co. H
Humphries, J.L. ~ Co. H
Humphries, Lawson ~ Co. H
Humphries, Oliver ~ Co. H
Hunsucker, Lawson ~ Co. C
Hunt, Joseph ~ Co. H
Hunter, John ~ Co. G
Hunter, R.B. ~ Co. G
Huss, Jacob ~ Co. K
Hyde, John S. ~ Co. B
Ijames, William J. ~ Co. A
Insenhour, J.A. ~ Co. F
Ireland, Amos ~ Co. D
Isenhaur, Isaac ~ Co. C
Jackson, William F. ~ Co. A
Jacobs, William W. ~ Co. B
Jameson, John E. ~ Co. B
Jenkins, Berryman ~ Co. E
Johnson, A.L. ~ Co. C
Johnson, A.R. ~ Co. K
Johnson, J.H. ~ Co. G
Johnson, J.L. ~ Co. G
Johnson, William A. ~ Co. G
Jonas, John ~ Co. K
Jones, Cullen ~ Co. A
Jones, I. J. ~ Co. H
Jones, P. L. ~ Co. A

Jones, Samuel ~ Co. A
Jones, Spencer ~ Co. A
Jordan, George ~ Co. G
Judden, George ~ Co. G
Justice, Benjamin ~ Co. H
Justice, John ~ Co. H
Kahill, Daniel ~ Co. C
Kale, Henderson ~ Co. C
Kanipe, Adam ~ Co. K
Kanipe, David ~ Co. K
Kanipe, Joseph ~ Co. K
Keaton, Silas ~ Co. D
Keener, Daniel ~ Co. C
Keener, Lewis ~ Co. K
Kelley, A. J. ~ Co. K
Kendrick, Thomas ~ Co. H
Kennerly, J. P. ~ Co. D
Kerfeese, C. S. ~ Co. A
Kerfeese, Martin ~ Co. A
Kesler, Tobias ~ Co. B
Kimball, H.M. ~ Co. D
Kimball, Thomas ~ Co. D
Kincade, Andrew J. ~ Co. B
King, C.H. ~ Co. D
King, J.H. ~ Co. K
Kirk, John ~ Co. G
Kiser, Erwin ~ Co. F
Kisiah, Thomas ~ Co. I
Kistler, Phillip ~ Co. K
Klutz, Simeon ~ Co. B
Klutz, Solomon ~ Co. B
Knox, D.J.L. ~ Co. D
Knox, David F. ~ Co. B
Krider, George H. ~ Co. B
Krider, Leonard S. ~ Co. B
Lackey, John ~ Co. K
Ladford, C.E. ~ Co. H
Ladford, J.R. ~ Co. H
Lael, Jacob ~ Co. C
Lamb, Alexander ~ Co. B
Lambert, John C. ~ Co. A
Lamberth, John ~ Co. D
Lambirth, W.L. ~ Co. D

Lane, Duglass ~ Co. A
Laney, Neb O. ~ Co. I
Langston, William H. ~ Co. A
Lantham, T. ~ Co. D
Lare, Ephraim ~ Co. C
Lawing, Joseph ~ Co. G
Lawing, Thomas ~ Co. G,K
Lawrence, Levi ~ Co. B
Lawson, R.E. ~ Co. D
Lazenberry, E.P. ~ Co. D
Lazenberry, H.B. ~ Co. D
Lazenberry, R.M. ~ Co. D
Leach, L. ~ Co. D
Leazer, John W. ~ Co. B
Lefler, John A. ~ Co. A
Lefler, Thomas ~ Co. F
Lemmond, M.M. ~ Co. I
Lenty, D. ~ Co. D
Leonhardt, Lawrance ~ Co. K
Leutz, P. J. ~ Co. F
Lewis, James ~ Co. E
Liles, David H. ~ Co. I
Linebarger, H.H. ~ Co. C
Lineberger, Jonas R. ~ Co. E
Linfield, J.W. ~ Co. B
Linfield, James ~ Co. B
Link, John W. ~ Co. B
Linn, Archebald ~ Co. C
Linn, John ~ Co. F
Litaker, Michael ~ Co. B
Lockhart, William ~ Co. E
Lofton, Joel ~ Co. Unknown
Long, Adam ~ Co. I
Long, G. A. ~ Co. I
Long, Jacob ~ Co. I
Long, Peter ~ Co. B
Lore, Ephraim ~ Co. K
Love, Ephraim ~ Co. K
Love, F. G. ~ Co. C
Lovelace, Asa ~ Co. H
Lowder, Mathias ~ Co. A
Lowrance, M. C. ~ Co. E
Lucas, Peter ~ Co. H

Lyerly, C. ~ Co. D
Lyerly, George M. ~ Co. B
Lyerly, William A. ~ Co. B
Lynn, Archibald ~ Co. C,K
Lytaker, Michael ~ Co. B
Magness, Robert ~ Co. H
Mahaley, Jesse A. ~ Co. B
Manney, John ~ Co. E
Marshall, John ~ Co. C
Marshall, William ~ Co. K
Martin, Andrew ~ Co. H
Martin, E. L. ~ Co. F
Martin, E. R. ~ Co. F
Mason, T. M. ~ Co. D
Mass, Edward ~ Co. F
Mathiason, Henry ~ Co. D
Matthews, Levi ~ Co. C
Matthews, Peter ~ Co. C
Mayer, R. M. ~ Co. D
Mayes, Rufus W. ~ Co. D
McAlister, David ~ Co. E
McAlister, Elisha ~ Co. E
McCall, J. A. ~ Co. G
McCall, Sylvester ~ Co. I
McCarver, Eli ~ Co. E
McClelland, J. M. ~ Co. D
McClemmer, George ~ Co. C
McConnell, Thomas ~ Co. D
McCorkle, G. R. ~ Co. D
McCorkle, William H. ~ Co. G
McCraney, J. M. ~ Co. G
McCrarry, John S. ~ Co. D
McCrary, T. F. ~ Co. D
McCraw, Robert ~ Co. H
McCulloh, James ~ Co. A
McDaniel, Joseph ~ Co. A
McDaniel, William ~ Co. H
McElwain, John ~ Co. E
McEntire, William ~ Co. H
McGinis, E. P. ~ Co. G
McIlvane, John ~ Co. E
McIntosh, A. ~ Co. G
McKibbon, A. J. ~ Co. F

McKibbon, R. L. ~ Co. F
McKiney, James ~ Co. H
McKinney, Wesley ~ Co. G
McKnight, John ~ Co. B
McKnight, John M. ~ Co. G,K
McLaughlin, John H. ~ Co. B
McLean, John W. ~ Co. B
McLelland, James C. ~ Co. F
McLure, William C.D. ~ Co. E
McNair, James ~ Co. E
McNeely, J.E. ~ Co. D
McNeely, Robert A. ~ Co. G
McSwain, H. K. ~ Co. H
McSwain, W. B. ~ Co. H
Meadlock, Elijah ~ Co. C
Meggs, Jonathan ~ Co. I
Melchor, Daniel ~ Co. F
Menus, Henry ~ Co. B
Merill, David ~ Co. I
Merkin, J. ~ Co. D
Merril, Martin S. ~ Co. E
Miller, Charles ~ Co. B
Miller, George ~ Co. I
Miller, Jacob C. ~ Co. A
Miller, John ~ Co. B
Miller, Michael ~ Co. B
Miller, Paul ~ Co. F
Miller, W.F. ~ Co. C
Miller, W.G. ~ Co. D
Miller, William ~ Co. A
Mills, William J. ~ Co. B
Miner, John ~ Co. D
Mingus, Miles ~ Co. C
Minish, J. C. ~ Co. D
Misenhcimcr, M. ~ Co. D
Monteith, Abner ~ Co. D
Mooney, Daniel ~ Co. H
Mooney, David ~ Co. H
Mooney, John ~ Co. E
Moore, Alexander ~ Co. G
Moore, James ~ Co. I
Moore, Robert ~ Co. D
Moorehead, E. J. ~ Co. H

Moose, John ~ Co. F
Morgan, Jacob ~ Co. B
Morgan Jr., Wiley ~ Co. B
Morgan Sr., Wiley ~ Co. B
Morrison, D. J. ~ Co. H
Morrison, F. ~ Co. D
Morrison, John L. ~ Co. B
Morrison, Pinkney ~ Co. F
Morrison, Robert H. ~ Co. F
Morrison, Thomas G. ~ Co. D
Morrison, William F. ~ Co. D
Morrison, William P. ~ Co. E
Morrisson, Evan T. ~ Co. E
Morrisson, John ~ Co. E
Morrow, J. A. ~ Co. G
Morrow, Stephen ~ Co. D
Moss, Edward ~ Co. H
Moss, Martin ~ Co. H
Mowery, Alexander ~ Co. B
Mullis, Williams ~ Co. D
Mulls, Calvin ~ Co. I
Mumford, G. E. ~ Co. A
Murph, Jeffrey ~ Co. B
Murphy, Basil ~ Co. A
Myars, James ~ Co. D
Myers, Daniel ~ Co. F
Myers, Jeremiah ~ Co. D
Myers, John ~ Co. A
Myers, Rufus W. ~ Co. D
Naylor, John W. ~ Co. A
Neely, John S. ~ Co. G
Neil, W. S. ~ Co. D
Nelson, J. B. ~ Co. A
Nicholson, E. ~ Co. D
Nims, Harris ~ Co. E
Noles, David ~ Co. K
Noles, W. P. ~ Co. G
Noles, W. R. ~ Co. K
Nothey, James ~ Co. G
Nusman, Sol ~ Co. F
Ochler (Ockler), George F. ~ Co. F
Ochler, John ~ Co. G
Oglesby, S. ~ Co. G

Orrell, James ~ Co. A
Overcash, Caleb ~ Co. D
Overcash, J. ~ Co. F
Overcash, James ~ Co. D
Overcash, Leonard ~ Co. B
Overcash, S. ~ Co. D
Overcash, William ~ Co. D
Owens, Joel ~ Co. A
Pace, Abner ~ Co. B
Page, William ~ Co. B
Pahel, John ~ Co. B, G
Parham, H. C. ~ Co. F
Parker, A. ~ Co. D
Parker, William ~ Co. I
Parks, Mack ~ Co. A
Parrish, David L. ~ Co. F
Parsons, J. B. ~ Co. A
Pasour, Felix ~ Co. E
Pasten, Thomas ~ Co. D
Patterson, F. A. ~ Co. H
Patterson, J. M. ~ Co. H
Patterson, R. M. ~ Co. K
Paysbur, J. W. ~ Co. K
Peeber, George H. ~ Co. B
Peeler, J. H. ~ Co. H
Pendergrass, Jesse ~ Co. G
Penglase, Richard ~ Co. E
Penniger, Nelson ~ Co. B
Perry, Joseph ~ Co. D
Pethel, John ~ Co. B
Pethel, Levi A. ~ Co. B
Petrea, Augustus ~ Co. B
Petrie, Augustus ~ Co. B
Petry, Lawson ~ Co. K
Pheifer, A. J. ~ Co. I
Pheifer, Elisha ~ Co. I
Pheifer, John E. ~ Co. I
Phifer, George L. ~ Co. F
Phillips, Andrew J. ~ Co. B
Phillips, Harvey ~ Co. F
Phillips, Robert ~ Co. I
Pickler, A. F. ~ Co. A
Plonk, David ~ Co. E

Plunk, David ~ Co. E
Plyler, Hugh ~ Co. D
Plyler, L. ~ Co. D
Pool, Edward ~ Co. B
Poovey, Emanuel ~ Co. C
Pope, Aman ~ Co. C
Porter, J. L. ~ Co. G
Porter, J. N. ~ Co. I
Porter, James M. ~ Co. K
Posten (Poston), John E. ~ Co. D
Powlass, John ~ Co. B
Presley, Andrew ~ Co. A
Presley, Eli ~ Co. I
Price, Ransom ~ Co. H
Price, Robert ~ Co. H
Prior, John N. ~ Co. Unknown
Privett, Martin ~ Co. I
Privy, Joseph ~ Co. D
Proctor, Richard ~ Co. K
Propst, Ales ~ Co. C
Propst, Avery ~ Co. C
Propst, George A. ~ Co. F
Propst, Michael ~ Co. C
Proptr, Michael ~ Co. K
Queen, Mitchel ~ Co. A
Quinn, Martin ~ Co. H
Ramsey, Jacob ~ Co. E
Ramsey, W. R. ~ Co. I
Ramsur, D. W. ~ Co. K
Ramsy, William H. ~ Co. D
Rankin, Robert ~ Co. E
Ransey, Jacob ~ Co. E
Rea, John K. ~ Co. G
Rea, Lee ~ Co. G
Reed, John L. ~ Co. F
Reep, Daniel ~ Co. K
Reid, J. Y. ~ Co. K,G
Reid, James W. ~ Co. E
Reid, John ~ Co. G
Renager, Nathan ~ Co. D
Rex, William ~ Co. B
Rhodes, Caleb ~ Co. E
Rhodes, Joseph ~ Co. E

Rhoney, John G. ~ Co. C
Rhyne, Adam A. ~ Co. E
Rhyne, Jacob H. (K.) ~ Co. E
Rice, Stewart ~ Co. I
Richardson, Columbus ~ Co. A
Richardson, J. F. ~ Co. I
Richardson, M. J. ~ Co. I
Ridenhour, E.N. ~ Co. F
Riggins, Charles D. ~ Co. I
Rimer, Caleb ~ Co. B
Rinehart, Matthias ~ Co. F
Rinehart, Paul ~ Co. F
Rippy, James ~ Co. H
Roane, L.K. ~ Co. I
Roark, R.M. ~ Co. H
Roberts, J. M. ~ Co. G
Roberts, Michael ~ Co. E
Robertson, Andrew ~ Co. K
Robinson, Elam ~ Co. G,K
Robinson, Harvey ~ Co. G
Rogers, Calvin ~ Co. I
Rogers, S. K. ~ Co. F
Rogers, W. P. ~ Co. F
Rohm, David ~ Co. E
Rone, Loyd K. ~ Co. I
Roseman, James O. ~ Co. B
Ross, J. C. ~ Co. G
Ross, Mathew ~ Co. H
Rouk, Jesse ~ Co. K
Rudasil, Jonas ~ Co. G
Ruffield, George ~ Co. K
Rusher, Milas ~ Co. B,D
Rusher, Miles ~ Co. B,D
Rushing, Green B. ~ Co. I
Russell, D. G. ~ Co. I
Rutledge, Robert ~ Co. E
Rymer, Caleb ~ Co. B
Sain, Chesire ~ Co. A
Sain, Jacob ~ Co. K
Salmon, Elisha ~ Co. L
Sanders, Slmpson ~ Co. E
Saunders, Jesse ~ Co. G
Scofield, J.N. ~ Co. D

Scott, A.M. ~ Co. D
Seaford, Simeon ~ Co. A
Seamont, James ~ Co. A
Secrest, Samuel T. ~ Co. I
Seitz, D.D. ~ Co. C
Settine, Emanuel ~ Co. K
Setzer, David ~ Co. C
Setzer, James H. ~ Co. C
Sharp, James ~ Co. G
Sharpe, David ~ Co. D
Shaver, Daniel ~ Co. B
Shepperd, James A. ~ Co. B
Sherford, Daniel D. ~ Co. B
Sherrill, J.S. ~ Co. C
Sherrill, James ~ Co. C, K
Shinn, John L. ~ Co. F
Shipping, Moses ~ Co. B,G
Shoaf, Alexander ~ Co. B
Shook, Daniel ~ Co. C
Shook, David ~ Co. C
Shook, Jacob ~ Co. C
Shronce, S.R. ~ Co. K
Shrum, Michael ~ Co. E
Shuford, Max ~ Co. C
Shuping, Caleb ~ Co. B
Shuping, Moses ~ Co. B,G
Sigman, Abel ~ Co. C
Sigman, David ~ Co. C
Sigman, Emanuel ~ Co. C
Sigman, Lanson ~ Co. C
Simerel, T. J. ~ Co. G
Simmon, Daniel ~ Co. C
Simmon, Joel ~ Co. C
Simpson, David ~ Co. I
Simpson, Jackson ~ Co. I
Simpson, Jefferson ~ Co. G
Sinclair, D. A. ~ Co. I
Sloan, Samuel ~ Co. A
Smith, Anderson W. ~ Co. A
Smith, Andrew ~ Co. E
Smith, Ed ~ Co. G
Smith, Elijah ~ Co. E
Smith, Henry ~ Co. E

Smith, J. A. ~ Co. A
Smith, J. E. W. ~ Co. I
Smith, L. G. ~ Co. A
Smith, Marcus M. ~ Co. C
Smith, Martin ~ Co. K
Smith, Paul B. C. ~ Co. F
Smith, S. O. ~ Co. A
Smith, Thomas ~ Co. H
Smith, William ~ Co. A
Sneed, James ~ Co. K
Snider, D. ~ Co. D
Snyder, Daniel ~ Co. D
Soserman, William ~ Co. G
Sossaman, H. M. ~ Co. B
Sossaman, John C. ~ Co. F
Sowrey, Adam ~ Co. K
Spake, Sam ~ Co. K
Sparks, Alpheus ~ Co. H
Speagle, Emanuel ~ Co. C
Spencer, Eli ~ Co. C
Springs, Alexander ~ Co. K
Springs, E. A. ~ Co. G
Springs, J. M. ~ Co. G
Sprinkle, Moses ~ Co. D
Spry, Lemuel ~ Co. A
Spry, William ~ Co. A
Stack, J. ~ Co. D
Stack, Jerry ~ Co. D
Stanferd, M. P. ~ Co. G
Steele, James ~ Co. D
Stephenson, W. S. ~ Co. D
Sterritt, James L. ~ Co. B
Stewart, A. A. ~ Co. G
Stewart, Archibald ~ Co. K
Stewart, William ~ Co. G
Stigall, A. B. ~ Co. I
Stigall, J. B. ~ Co. I
Stirewalt, Adam ~ Co. B
Stirewalt, Jacob ~ Co. F
Stisewalt, Paul ~ Co. F
Stone, John ~ Co. E
Stowe, Henry M. ~ Co. F
Stowe, Leroy W. ~ Co. Unknown

Stowe, Levi ~ Co. F
Strickland, John ~ Co. I
Strong, John M. ~ Co. G
Stroup, J.E. ~ Co. E
Sulliman, John P. ~ Co. B
Sullivan, J.W. ~ Co. H
Summers, B.F. ~ Co. D
Summerville, Robert J. ~ Co. E
Suther, A.M. ~ Co. F
Swanner, J.M. ~ Co. I
Tanner, H. ~ Co. D
Tate, Asa ~ Co. H
Tatum, E.W. ~ Co. A
Taylor, John ~ Co. A
Thompson, Henry ~ Co. D
Thompson, S.T. ~ Co. I
Thornburg, Daniel ~ Co. E
Thornburg, William ~ Co. E
Thrap, Thomas ~ Co. D
Tiege, William ~ Co. E
Tisenger, Peter ~ Co. A
Tom, D.C. ~ Co. D
Tomberlin, Durias ~ Co. I
Tomlin, J.H. ~ Co. D
Traley, Thomas D. ~ Co. B
Traulman, Peter ~ Co. F
Trexler, Moses ~ Co. B
Trott, Jackson ~ Co. B
Tucker, Darling ~ Co. F
Tucker, J.B. ~ Co. H
Tucker, John F. ~ Co. F
Turner, B.S. ~ Co. C
Turner, R.B. ~ Co. H
Turner, Wiley ~ Co. H
Tutterow, H. ~ Co. A
Tutterow, Samuel ~ Co. A
Tutterow, W.W. ~ Co. A
Underwood, Willis ~ Co. G,K
Upright, John ~ Co. B
Upright, Samuel S. ~ Co. B
Upwright, John ~ Co. B
Urey, Levi ~ Co. F
Vaughn, A. ~ Co. D

Wafford, John ~ Co. F
Waggoner, John ~ Co. B
Wagoner, J.L. ~ Co. D
Wagoner, John ~ Co. F
Wagoner, Len F. ~ Co. D
Walice, James ~ Co. G
Walker, T.E. ~ Co. A
Walker, William ~ Co. D
Wallace, J.C. ~ Co. D
Wallace, John N. ~ Co. G
Wallace, M.A. ~ Co. F
Wallis, David ~ Co. H
Wallis, J.Y. ~ Co. H
Walter, A. ~ Co. F
Ware, A.B. ~ Co. H
Waring, Robert P. ~ Co. F&S
Watt, Eron ~ Co. G
Watts, J. A. ~ Co. D
Waugh, B. A. ~ Co. D
Weatherman, Henry H. ~ Co. D
Weaver, Esau ~ Co. F
Weaver, Esrom ~ Co. F
Weaver, John M. ~ Co. B
Weddington, R. H. ~ Co. G
Westmoreland, ~ Co. D
Wharton, J. ~ Co. D
White, Alex ~ Co. D
White, B. ~ Co. D
Whitehead, Jesse ~ Co. D
Whitener, A. J. ~ Co. C
Whitener, Abel ~ Co. C
Whitener, Z. B. ~ Co. C
Whitesides, Edward ~ Co. E
Whitesides, S. M. ~ Co. G
Whitt, J. W. ~ Co. H
Wilburn, H. D. A. ~ Co. K
Wiley, J. R. ~ Co. H
Wilhelm, A. D. ~ Co. D
Wilhelm, Henry ~ Co. B
Wilkson, D. ~ Co. D
Willtord, W. H. ~ Co. D
Williams, Alex. ~ Co. D
Williams, Isaac ~ Co. A

Williams, John ~ Co. B
Williams, M. ~ Co. D
Williams, Martin ~ Co. A
Williams, S. ~ Co. D
Willson, D. C. ~ Co. A
Wilson, Maxwell ~ Co. K
Wilson, S. S. ~ Co. G
Winecoff, Daniel ~ Co. F
Winecoff, Henry ~ Co. F
Winecoff, Vol ~ Co. F
Wolfe, J. H. ~ Co. G
Wood, H. S. ~ Co. H
Wood, T. W. ~ Co. H

Woodring, Joseph ~ Co. C
Woodruff, William L. ~ Co. B
Woods, T.L. ~ Co. F
Wooton, J. ~ Co. D
Wooton, L. W. ~ Co. D
Wright, John L. ~ Co. A
Wright, Nathan ~ Co. H
Wright, W. ~ Co. D
Wyckoff, Abraham (Abram) ~ Co. C
Yandell, Sherwood ~ Co. I
Yaunt, F. A. ~ Co. C
Yorborough, G. W. M. ~ Co. I
Yost, Aaron ~ Co. F

For Further Research

The website links referenced in this appendix change periodically. Check our website for updates.

http://www.researchonline.net/linkupdates.htm

National Archives and Records Administration

http://www.archives.gov/research/order/order-vets-records.html

Confederate Records

http://www.archives.gov/research/military/civil-war/

For Confederate army soldiers, there are two major record collections in the National Archives and Records Administration that provide information on military service:

(1) compiled military service record (CMSR) and

(2) records reproduced in microfilm publication M861, *Compiled Records Showing Service of Military Units in Confederate Organizations* (74 rolls). Records relating to Confederate soldiers are typically less complete than those relating to Union soldiers because many Confederate records did not survive the war. These records are now available on CD-ROM by state. They may be ordered from our website for $35.00 per state.

http://www.researchonline.net/catalog/service.htm

NARA does not have pension files for Confederate soldiers. Pensions were granted to Confederate veterans and their widows and minor children by the States of Alabama, Arkansas, Florida, Georgia, Kentucky, Louisiana, Mississippi, Missouri, North Carolina, Oklahoma, South Carolina, Tennessee, Texas, and Virginia; these records are in the state archives or equivalent agency.

NARA records are available from the Family History Library in Salt Lake City Utah. You can order them at your local Family History Center (FHC) (Mormon Church). The centers should have a Research Outline on Military Records which should cost about a dollar. Also there is a good book out on Military Records (NARA) by James Neagle. It should be in most FHC. In the card catalog on microfiche, you can go to the Author/Title section, look under Author = National Archives. All their film is there listed by NARA # (sample - M530. LDS microfilm is quicker and cheaper than requesting from NARA}.

To obtain Civil War military service and pension records by mail

Paper copies of Civil War military service and pension records can be ordered by mail using one NATF Form 80 for **each soldier** and **each type of file**.

You can obtain the NATF Form 80 by providing your name and mailing address to inquire@nara.gov. Be sure to specify "Form 80" and the number of forms you need.

You can also obtain the NATF Form 80 by writing to:

National Archives and Records Administration
Attn: NWDT1
700 Pennsylvania Avenue, NW
Washington, DC 20408-0001

The Cost of this type of lookup is $45.00.

CONFEDERATE SERVICE AND PENSION RECORDS

The agencies listed below are repositories for Confederate pension records. The veteran was eligible to apply for a pension to the State in which he lived, even if he served in a unit from a different State. Generally, an applicant was eligible for a pension only if he was indigent or disabled. In your letter to the repository, state the Confederate veteran's name, his widow's name, the unit(s) in which he served, and the counties in which he and his widow lived after the Civil War. Some repositories also have records of Confederate Homes (for veterans, widows, etc.), muster rolls of State Confederate militia, and other records related to the war. For information on procedures and fees for requesting copies of records, contact the appropriate repository. Also See Online Pension Indexes for Florida, Georgia, Tennessee, Texas and Virginia

ALABAMA

Alabama Department of Archives and History –

http://www.archives.state.al.us/index.html

624 Washington Avenue
Montgomery, AL 36130-0100
Telephone: 334-242-4363

A Guide to Alabama Civil War Research is available in EBOOK and paper formats. 211 pgs.

http://www.researchonline.net/catalog/110601.htm

In 1867 Alabama began granting pensions to Confederate veterans who had lost arms or legs. In 1886 the State began granting pensions to veterans' widows. In 1891 the law was amended to grant pensions to indigent veterans or their widows.

Service records of Alabama soldiers may be viewed on line:

http://archives.state.al.us/civilwar/search.cfm

ARKANSAS

Arkansas History Commission and State Archives

http://www.ark-ives.com/

1 Capitol Mall
Little Rock, AR 72201
Telephone: 501-682-6900

In 1891 Arkansas began granting pensions to indigent Confederate veterans. In 1915 the State began granting pensions to their widows and mothers.

Two published indexes are available in many libraries:

Allen, Desmond Walls. Index to Confederate Pension Applications (Conway, Ark.: Arkansas Research, 1991).

Ingmire, Frances Terry. Arkansas Confederate Veterans and Widows Pensions Applications (St. Louis, MO: F.T. Ingmire, 1985).

FLORIDA

Florida State Archives –

http://dlis.dos.state.fl.us/index_researchers.cfm

R. A. Gray Building
500 South Bronough Street
Tallahassee, FL 32399-0250
Telephone: 850.245.6700

In 1885 Florida began granting pensions to Confederate veterans. In 1889 the State began granting pensions to their widows.

A published index, which provides each veteran's pension number, is available in many libraries:

White, Virgil. Register of Florida CSA Pension Applications (Waynesboro, TN: National Historical Publishing Co., 1989).

GEORGIA

Georgia Department of Archives and History –

http://www.georgiaarchives.org/

Georgia State Archives
5800 Jonesboro Rd.
Morrow, GA 30260
Telephone: 678-364-3700

A Guide to Georgia Civil War Research is available in EBOOK and paper formats. 211 pgs.

http://www.researchonline.net/catalog/090801.htm

In 1870 Georgia began granting pensions to soldiers with artificial limbs. In 1879 the State began granting pensions to other disabled Confederate veterans or their widows who then resided in Georgia. By 1894 eligible disabilities had been expanded to include old age and poverty.

A published index is available in many libraries:

> *White, Virgil D.* Index to Georgia Civil War Confederate Pension Files (Waynesboro, TN: National Historical Publishing Co., 1996). and online:

KENTUCKY

Kentucky State Archives –

http://www.kdla.ky.gov/

Research Room
300 Coffee Tree Road
Frankfort, KY 40601

Telephone: 502-564-8300

In 1912, Kentucky began granting pensions to Confederate veterans or their widows. The records are on microfilm. A published index is available in many libraries:

> *Simpson, Alicia.* Index of Confederate Pension Applications, Commonwealth of Kentucky (Frankfort, KY: Division of Archives and Records Management, Department of Library and Archives, 1978).

LOUISIANA

Louisiana State Archives –

http://www.sos.la.gov/Pages/default.aspx

3851 Essen Lane
Baton Rouge, LA 70809-2137
Telephone: 225-922-1000

In 1898 Louisiana began granting pensions to indigent Confederate veterans or their widows.

MISSISSIPPI

Mississippi State Archives –

http://www.mdah.state.ms.us/

Mississippi Department of Archives and History

P.O. Box 571

Jackson, MS 39205
Telephone: 601- 576-6850

In 1888 Mississippi began granting pensions to indigent Confederate veterans or their widows. A published index is available in many libraries:

> *Wiltshire, Betty C.* Mississippi Confederate Pension Applications (Carrollton, MS: Pioneer Publishing Co., 1994).

MISSOURI

Missouri State Archives –

http://www.sos.mo.gov/archives/

State Information Center
300 West Main Street
P.O. Box 1747
Jefferson City, MO 65102
Telephone: 573-751-3280

In 1911 Missouri began granting pensions to indigent Confederate veterans only; none were granted to widows. Missouri also had a home for disabled Confederate veterans. The pension and veterans' home applications are interfiled and arranged alphabetically. Typically, the pension file is small, perhaps four to eight pages, containing a standard application form and may include letters of recommendation from family members or others.

NORTH CAROLINA

North Carolina Department of Cultural Resources

Division of Archives and History –

http://www.ah.dcr.state.nc.us/

109 East Jones Street
Raleigh, NC 27601-2807
Telephone: 919-733-7305

In 1867 North Carolina began granting pensions to Confederate veterans who were blinded or lost an arm or leg during their service. In 1885 the State began granting pensions to all other disabled indigent Confederate veterans or widows.

OKLAHOMA

Archives and Records Management Divisions –

http://www.odl.state.ok.us/oar/archives/collections.htm

200 Northeast 18th Street
Oklahoma City, OK 73105
Telephone: (405) 522-3579

In 1915 Oklahoma began granting pensions to Confederate veterans or their widows. A published index is available in many libraries:

Oklahoma Genealogical Society. Index to Applications for Pensions from the State of Oklahoma, Submitted by Confederate Soldiers, Sailors, and Their Widows

(Oklahoma City, OK: Oklahoma Genealogical Society Projects Committee, 1969)

SOUTH CAROLINA

South Carolina Department of Archives and History

http://scdah.sc.gov/

8301 Parklane Road
Columbia, SC 29223
Telephone: 803-896-6100

A Guide to South Carolina Civil War Research is available in EBOOK and paper formats. 200 pgs.

http://www.researchonline.net/catalog/scresearch.htm

A state law enacted December 24, 1887, permitted financially needy Confederate veterans and widows to apply for a pension; however, few applications survive from the 1888-1918 era. Beginning in 1889, the SC Comptroller began publishing lists of such veterans receiving pensions in his Annual Report. To obtain a copy of the pension application from the 1888-1918 era, the researcher needs to know the exact year in which the veteran or widow applied for a pension. From 1919 to 1925, South Carolina granted pensions to Confederate veterans and widows regardless of financial need. These files are arranged alpha-betically. Pension application files are typically one sheet of paper with writing on both sides. Also available are Confederate Home applications and inmate records for veterans (1909-

1957), and applications of wives, widows, sisters, and daughters (1925-1955).

TENNESSEE

Tennessee State Library and Archives –

http://sos.tn.gov/tsla

Public Service Division
403 Seventh Avenue North
Nashville, TN 37243-0312
Telephone: 615-741-2764

A Guide to Tennessee Civil War Research is available in EBOOK and paper formats. 180 pgs.

http://www.researchonline.net/catalog/110801.htm

In 1891 Tennessee began granting pensions to indigent Confederate veterans. In 1905 the State began granting pensions to their widows. The records are on microfilm.

A published index is available in many libraries:

Sistler, Samuel. Index to Tennessee Confederate Pension Applications (Nashville, TN: Sistler & Assoc., 1995).

Confederate Home records are also available, and there is an online index:

Index to Tennessee Confederate Soldiers' Home Applications

http://www.tennessee.gov/tsla/history/military/pension.htm

TEXAS

Texas State Library and Archives Commission –

http://www.tsl.state.tx.us/

P.O. Box 12927
Austin, TX 78711
Telephone: 512-463-5480

In 1881 Texas set aside 1,280 acres for disabled Confederate veterans. In 1889 the State began granting pensions to indigent Confederate veterans and their widows. Muster rolls of State militia in Confederate service are also available.

A published index is available in many libraries:

White, Virgil D. Index to Texas CSA Pension Files (Waynesboro, TN: National Historical Publishing Co., 1989).

An online Index:

Index to Texas Confederate Pension Applications, 1899-1975

http://www.tsl.state.tx.us/arc/pensions/introcpi.html

VIRGINIA

Library of Virginia –

http://www.lva.lib.va.us

Archives Division
800 East Broad Street
Richmond, VA 23219
Telephone: 804-692-3500

In 1888 Virginia began granting pensions to Confederate veterans or their widows. The records are on microfilm. Two indexes are available online:

Virginia Confederate Pension Rolls (Veterans and Widows) Database

http://lva1.hosted.exlibrisgroup.com/F/?file_name=find-b-clas10&func=file&local_base=CLAS10

The Historical Sketch & Roster Series

These books contain information for researching the men who served in a particular unit. The focus is for genealogical rather than historical research. More than 1100 volumes are currently available. For a complete listing see our website:

For Confederate Titles by State

http://www.researchonline.net/catalog/crhmast.htm

For Union Titles by State

http://www.researchonline.net/catalog/urhmast.htm

TABLE OF CONTENTS:

List of Officers with biographical sketches
List of companies and the counties where formed
Officers of each company
Military assignments
Battles engaged in the war
Historical sketch of the regiment's service
Rosters / compiled service records of each company
Bibliography of sources

Paperback - $25.00 (Selected larger volumes are more expensive.)

CD-ROM - $15.00

EBOOK - $9.49 – PDF format of the book delivered by EMAIL – NO SHIPPING CHARGE

Shipping is $6.00 per order regardless of the number of titles ordered.

Order From:

Eastern Digital Resources
31 Bramblewood Drive SW
Cartersville, GA 30120
(678) 739-9177
Order on Line
http://www.researchonline.net/catalog/crhmast.htm
Sales@researchonline.net

Made in the USA
Columbia, SC
06 February 2022

55556097R00070